Reaching Out

A Musician's Guide
To
Interactive Performance

David Wallace

Mc Graw Hill

Boston   Burr Ridge, IL   Dubuque, IA   New York
San Francisco   St. Louis   Bangkok   Bogotá   Caracas   Kuala Lumpur
Lisbon   London   Madrid   Mexico City   Milan   Montreal   New Delhi
Santiago   Seoul   Singapore   Sydney   Taipei   Toronto

Higher Education

Published by McGraw-Hill, an imprint of The McGraw-Hill Companies, Inc., 1221 Avenue of the Americas, New York, NY 10020. Copyright © 2008. All rights reserved. No part of this publication may be reproduced or distributed in any form or by any means, or stored in a database or retrieval system, without the prior written consent of The McGraw-Hill Companies, Inc., including, but not limited to, in any network or other electronic storage or transmission, or broadcast for distance learning.

2 3 4 5 6 7 8 9 0 EUS/EUS 0 9 8

ISBN: 978-0-07-340138-6
MHID: 0-07-340138-2

Editor in Chief: *Emily Barrosse*
Publisher: *Lisa Moore*
Sponsoring Editor: *Chris Freitag*
Marketing Manager: *Pamela Cooper*
Editorial Assistant: *Marley Magaziner*
Project Manager: *Amanda Peabody*
Design Manager: *Andrei Pasternak*
Production Supervisor: *Tandra Jorgensen*
Composition: *10/12 Sabon by ICC Macmillan Inc.*
Printing: *60# Opaque, Quebecor World Eusey*

Credits: *Cover photo – Michael DiVito*

Library of Congress Cataloging-in-Publication Data
Wallace, David, 1970-
  Reaching out : a musician's guide to interactive performance / David Wallace. — 1st ed.
    p. cm.
  Includes bibliographical references (p.).
  ISBN-13: 978-0-07-340138-6
  ISBN-10: 0-07-340138-2
  1. Music audiences—Psychological aspects.   2. Music—Performance.   3. Concerts.   I. Title.
ML3838.W24 2008
781.4'3—dc22
                                                                    2007013505

The Internet addresses listed in the text were accurate at the time of publication. The inclusion of a Web site does not indicate an endorsement by the authors or McGraw-Hill, and McGraw-Hill does not guarantee the accuracy of the information presented at these sites.

#122973544

www.mhhe.com

Contents

Acknowledgments

I owe a tremendous debt of gratitude to . . .

My loving family: my sister Sheryl for providing the west-Texas writer's retreat that made this book a reality; my mother Marilyn for giving me a love of language; my father Charlie for introducing me to the joy of music; my wife Lauri for her love and steadfast belief in my work.

The mentors and teachers who have shaped my philosophy and approach: Dr. Edward Bilous and Eric Booth of the Juilliard School; Thomas Cabaniss of the Philadelphia Orchestra; Polly Kahn of the American Symphony Orchestra League; and Hilary Easton, Jean Taylor, and Cathryn Williams of the Lincoln Center Institute.

The wonderful people at the McGraw-Hill Companies who have generously supported this project: Chris Freitag, Louis Haber, Jenny Katsoros, Amanda Peabody and Ed Stanford.

The American Symphony Orchestra League for encouraging this project from its inception.

The concert presenters, educators, and benefactors who have embraced my ideas or encouraged my endeavors, especially: Lester and Dinny Morse; Kay Churchill and Chris Silva of the Bardavon 1869 Opera House and the Hudson Valley Philharmonic; Marya Martin and Ken Davidson of the Bridgehampton Chamber Music Festival; Dr. Joseph Polisi, Dr. Aaron Flagg, Dr. Laurie Carter, Alison Scott-Williams, and Robert Sherman of the Juilliard School; Rebecca Charnow of the Manhattan School of Music; Ellen Highstein of the Tanglewood Music Center; Jessica Balboni, Karl Montevirgen, and Ed Barguiarena of the Los Angeles Philharmonic; Matthew Loden and Bridget Anderson of Young Audiences of Houston; Richard Bell of Young Audiences, Inc.; Barb Day, Nancy Koepke, and Scott Seeburger of the Saginaw Community Enrichment Commission; Conductors Marietta Cheng, William Prinzing Briggs, and Alexander Mickelthwate; and Jon Deak, Kristen Houkom, Toya Lillard, Zarin Mehta, and Ted Wiprud of the New York Philharmonic.

The incredible Teaching Artists and teachers who have shaped and participated in this approach, especially: Daniel Levy and Dana Scofidio of The Doc Wallace Trio; Jessica Meyer; Gary Goldstein; and the incomparable Teaching Artist Faculty Ensemble of the New York

Philharmonic: Amy Sue Barston, Catherine Beeson, Richard Carrick, Janey Choi, Jennifer Choi, Kelly Dylla, Arnold Greenwich, Dr. Ani Gregorian, Judith Hill, Justin Hines, Sarah Skutel Holden, Sarah Johnson, Bridget Kibbey, Nora Kroll-Rosenbaum, Richard Mannoia, Misty Tolle Pereira, Paola Prestini, Rachel Shapiro, Dr. Airi Yoshioka, and Dr. Tanya Dusevic Witek.

Chamber Music America, Young Audiences, Inc., and the numerous orchestras and who have given me a platform for sharing my ideas.

The countless friends, colleagues, musicians, and teachers who believe and continue to contribute to this adventure.

About the Author

Photo credit: Daniel Levy

A faculty member of the Juilliard School and a Senior Teaching Artist at the New York Philharmonic, Dr. David Wallace enjoys a versatile career as a musician, composer, writer, and teaching artist. As a soloist, David has been broadcast on National Public Radio, PBS, CBS and ABC television, WQXR radio's McGraw-Hill Young Artist's Showcase, and the gospel music radio show *Live from the Lamb's*. David's concert performances include appearances with the Chamber Music Society of Lincoln Center, the Bridgehampton Chamber Music Festival, the Taos Chamber Music Festival, the New York Viola Society, Continuum, Music Unlocked!, and multi-instrumentalist and composer Mark O'Connor. David is also the violinist of the Texas-style string band The Doc Wallace Trio, which released its debut album, *Live at the Living Room*, in 2001 and which has performed educational concerts for Young Audiences of Houston, Young Audiences of New York, Midori & Friends, and the Lincoln Center Institute. As a composer, David has won awards from the ASCAP and the American Music Center. Recent comissions include a sextet for the New York Philharmonic and an electronic work for the Juliard School's centennial.

David has served as an educational consultant, workshop leader, and scriptwriter for numerous organizations, including the Tanglewood Music Festival, Chamber Music America, Meet the Composer, Young Audiences Inc., the New York Philharmonic, the Los Angeles Philharmonic, the Pittsburgh Symphony, the Virginia Symphony, the Hudson Valley Philharmonic, the Manhattan School of Music, the Eastman School of Music, and the American Symphony Orchestra League, for whom he has also served as a keynote session panelist. In 2002, David's numerous creative contributions were honored with the first annual $10,000 McGraw-Hill Companies' Robert Sherman Award for Music Education and Community Outreach, awarded to musicians who have distinguished themselves as artists and educators. David received his Doctor of Musical Arts with the Richard French Prize from the Juilliard School, where he served as teaching assistant to Karen Tuttle.

For Eric Booth,
who reaches further.

A Musical Quandary

During the winter of 1997, I wrestled with a musical quandary. I had just been offered a wonderful twenty-concert visiting artist's residency in Saginaw, Michigan, but I had to figure out a way to make it work with my repertoire. After all, not every audience immediately appreciates highly polyphonic Baroque works, Texas fiddling, or atonal, contemporary pieces. Amidst the excitement of planning the residency, my mind kept echoing the dubious refrains of concert-presenters and conductors who were considerably more cautious than my newfound friends in Saginaw:

"Kids just don't like classical music."
"I think you'd be better off if you presented a piece that told a story."
"You can't play any modern music on our series; we have to consider our
    subscription base."
"I really don't see how effective outreach can be done by just one *violist!*"

As much as I hated to think about these negative pronouncements, I had to admit that each statement was grounded in a stark reality. In order for my residency to succeed, I had to remove every barrier between me, my audience, and the music I loved. I needed a method for making the music come alive.

I spent the following months painstakingly figuring out how I could apply tried and true educational principles to a concert setting. The Juilliard School, the Lincoln Center Institute, and the New York Philharmonic had trained me in powerful methods of creative, experiential teaching that works wonders in long-term residencies, but could these methods work in a performance?

By the end of the residency, I could answer with a definitive "Yes!" In the process, I had gathered several new proclamations to replace the former ones:

"You play the best music I have ever heard."
    Dustin, fourth grade
"[The concert] was truly inspiring. So much that I have taken up private lessons
    again and am looking into attending Juilliard."
    Amal, tenth grade
"The song by J. S. Bach was cool."
    Andie-ah, fifth grade
"I have terminal cancer, and your concert just did me more good than all my
    chemotherapy treatments combined!"
    A seventy-year-old Episcopal priest

I had found a powerful way to share my music with the public I so fervently wanted to reach. I am writing this book so that you and other musicians can do the same.

By nature, any form of serious music may not be easily accessible or instantly gratifying to the broader public. Unfortunately, few people spend time learning to appreciate something that offers no immediate payoff. Moreover, in our multicultural, postmodern worldview, classical traditions have lost their elitist claims of being "superior music." Cultural and social status no longer provide significant motivations for attending concerts.

Clever marketing may draw new listeners to the concert halls, but audience members will return only if they are truly captivated by the concert experience itself. Our best recourse is to rethink the way we present our music.

This book presents a method for opening and heightening the perceptions of your audiences so that they are just as passionate about your music as you are. Most importantly, this method is grounded in the music itself, not marketing shenanigans or extramusical gimmicks. Various artists, ensembles, and orchestras have tested, refined, and contributed to this approach as it has developed. The ideas presented in this book represent contemporary practice, not just theory.

> If you are a serious musician who wants to give your audience a deeper experience of music, this book is for you.

Although many of my examples come from the experience of classical musicians, this method has worked for performers of jazz, bluegrass, Latin, folk, and other musical styles. If you are a serious musician who wants to give your audience a deeper experience of music, this book is for you. Let's go out and open some ears!

Dr. David Wallace
Halee and David Baldwin Teaching Artist Chair, the New York Philharmonic
Graduate Studies Faculty, the Juilliard School.

What Is an Interactive Performance?

*W*hat's an interactive performance?

"A concert where the performers talk."

Really? What do they talk about?

"They might say something about the composer or the music they're about to play. Sometimes they'll tell you something about their ensemble or instruments or say something funny about the group."

Oh. Does the audience get to do anything?

"Sure. In an interactive concert, they can always ask whatever they like at the end of the concert."

Hold it! Hold everything.

Unless I'm mistaken, the word "interact" implies that some sort of exchange is taking place. One person does something, which elicits a response from another person, which results in a new situation, which leads to another response, and the cycle continues. Cause and effect. Input-output. Give and take.

Interactive museum exhibits offer hands-on activity stations where visitors can learn by participating. Interactive computer games allow players to shape the direction and outcome of the game via continual conscious input. Interactive comedians invite audience members onstage to improvise skits with them.

In a world that is becoming increasingly interactive, why do so many musicians still think that an interactive performance is a concert where the performers talk and their silent, dutiful audience listens? If we publicize a performance as interactive, we must *interact*. Otherwise, let's call our event a lecture recital and stop kidding ourselves.

So what is an interactive performance? For the purposes of this book, let's assume the following definition:

> An interactive performance is an event where the performers help audience members to perform, create, and reflect in ways that heighten their musical perceptions.

An interactive performance is an event where the performers help audience members to perform, create, and reflect in ways that heighten their musical perceptions.

3

We can accomplish this objective through countless means. To illustrate a few possibilities, here are four successful musical interactions from actual concerts:

- A conductor teaches 2,000 audience members to perform along with the bass drum part to Aaron Copland's *Fanfare for the Common Man.*
- The leader of a jazz combo asks her audience to fill a hat with popular tune titles, which will be drawn by band members and quoted in their solos during the subsequent performance of "Sweet Georgia Brown"—the drummer promises a free CD to anyone whose selected quote isn't used!
- To introduce the unconventional musical language of George Crumb's *Black Angels*, a string quartet helps the audience to create a piece that uses strange sounds and extended string techniques to evoke "images from a dark land." After the performance, the audience compares its compositional decisions to Crumb's.
- Using introspective "actor's studio" questions, a violist leads his adult audience to reflect deeply on a personal grieving process and to express its emotions by humming a succession of consonant and dissonant harmonies prior to a performance of Igor Stravinsky's *Elegie.*

Now we're interacting! Do you see the difference? In each of these instances, the performers personally involve their audiences in ways that heighten their musical experiences. The performers are not merely sharing information or teaching listeners *about* the music, nor are they doing flashy, entertaining things that fail to tap the audience's musical intelligence. Rather, they are enabling the audience to enter the specific world of each piece.

The conductor simply could have prefaced his performance of *Fanfare for the Common Man* with a brief biography of Aaron Copland or a discussion of the work's history. But as an audience member, would receiving that information match the thrill of performing one of Copland's masterpieces with the Tanglewood Festival Orchestra?

The jazz musician could have explained quotation and told her audience to listen for familiar tunes. But would listeners feel the same excitement and payoff as when the band dared to let them have direct input into the solos?

Of course, real interaction entails a certain degree of risk. It might feel safer and easier just to talk. However, once you take the plunge and truly interact, you quickly discover that the payoffs far surpass any risks.

When you enable an audience to listen with a focused mind and active ears, there's a palpable electricity in the room. Nobody's daydreaming about what he's going to do after the concert. No one's critically comparing your interpretation to one she heard last fall. Everyone is focused on the music and the moment. Often, the audience will offer insights that may not have occurred to you, and your own perceptions of the music will deepen.

Heightened musical perception is the interactive performer's raison d'être. Such a performer learns to engage, educate, and entertain an audience, regardless of its demographic or level of musical expertise.

Interaction is more than a nice, extra touch for adding variety to our events; it is a vital component to the survival of serious music. To develop audiences, we must plan events that meet a growing demand for hands-on, audience-centered experiences. We need performances that draw new listeners into deeper levels of musical comprehension and satisfaction. We need musicians who can actively engage every listener in the house.

> Interaction is more than a nice, extra touch for adding variety to our events; it is a vital component to the survival of serious music.

Interactive performance meets these critical needs. And unlike many audience-development strategies, interactive performance is artistically grounded and fun. All it requires is the intelligent application of a few principles, strategies, and skills. Let's learn them!

Principles for Interactive Performance

Strong interactive performances are grounded in six general principles:

1. Give the audience an entry point.
2. Go beyond information and engage through experience.
3. Tap the competence of your audience.
4. Address multiple intelligences.
5. Reflect.
6. Project your personality in your performance.

Grounding your concerts in these principles will guarantee that your listeners stay connected to the music.

✇ PRINCIPLE #1: Give the Audience an Entry Point

Every piece of music contains elements that are central to its structure, meaning, and perception. When you sensitize listeners to one specific element, it becomes an entry point for listening actively and successfully.

You might think of an entry point as a compass for navigating the complexities of a musical work—or a key you give listeners to unlock a particular piece.

Because every musical work can be understood and perceived in a variety of ways, any given work has several potential entry points. For example, the first movement of Beethoven's Symphony No. 5 offers a variety of entry points: extreme dynamics, thematic contrast, suspense, orchestration, triumph, repetition, struggle, motives, thematic development, Beethoven's struggle with fate, and so on.

It is better to explore one specific entry point in depth than to offer a smorgasbord of entry points in hopes that listeners will latch onto one of them.

An effective presentation conveys how a particular entry point functions in the work. It is better to explore one specific entry point in depth than to offer a smorgasbord of entry points in hopes that listeners will latch onto one of them. Think about which aspect would most successfully hook your listeners. Choose an entry point that will focus them for the duration of the work.

A conductor presenting the Beethoven movement to young children might lead an activity where they repeatedly whisper, speak, or shout the opening theme in an exploration of how extreme dynamics generate suspense and excitement.

For an audience of high school band and orchestra students, a musician from the orchestra might shed some light on Beethoven's use of sonata form by helping the audience to compose and develop two contrasting themes. Another conductor might awaken her subscription audience to the way Beethoven develops themes through orchestration by singing the opening theme, then asking the audience to choose instruments for performing it in series. In each of these scenarios, listeners have been introduced to a specific entry point to the symphony, and their attention has been focused via a direct experience.

When we present entry points in this open, exploratory manner, listeners make their own discoveries as they listen. They go beyond merely identifying information we have given or demonstrated for them. This interactive application of an entry point is what jumpstarts the meaning-making process. *An entry point does not serve as well if we just talk about it.*

Jerry James, a visual artist and Teaching Artist for the Lincoln Center Institute, often relates arts appreciation approaches to the ways people can experience an ice-cream cone. If all we do is talk about an entry point, or our own interpretations of a work, it's like holding up an ice-cream cone and describing what eating it is like. When we give the audience a hands-on exploration of an entry point, we hand them an ice-cream cone and let them taste it for themselves. In all of the Beethoven examples, the presenters have transcended passive explanation by offering listeners a firsthand "taste" of one of Beethoven's musical ingredients.

Without a hands-on experience of an entry point, an uninitiated listener may find himself baffled, intimidated, or bored by complex or unfamiliar music. I distinctly remember my first encounter with Bartok string quartets as a sixteen-year-old audience member. Up until that point in my life, I had heard or studied only string quartets by Haydn, Mozart, Beethoven, Mendelssohn, Schubert, and Tchaikovsky. Largely unacquainted with twentieth-century musical language, I found Bartok's music dissonant, strident, raucous, and generally lacking melody and form. I concluded that Bartok was a horrible composer, and I became determined to avoid his music at all costs.

What went wrong that evening? In hindsight, I can't blame the performance— a famous quartet was clearly playing its heart out. Bartok's quartets are widely regarded as masterpieces, so this wasn't a case of poor repertoire.

Naive as I may have been about twentieth-century music, I was not an "ignorant, uncultured person who just needed more concert experience"; rather, I was a lifelong music lover and a serious violinist. Nevertheless, as hard as I tried, I found no way to listen successfully to the music. No matter how much the quartet or anyone else was enjoying the concert, I felt left out.

I needed an entry point. I needed someone to take me inside Bartok's musical mind and language so that I could understand the unfamiliar harmonies, timbres, and intervals.

Today Bartok's music makes perfect sense to me because I have had subsequent experience studying and performing it. However, my comfort with Bartok's music does not guarantee that my own audiences can successfully hear it. They will share my enjoyment only if they have an entry point.

By the same token, you must find ways to connect listeners to the music you love.

CONSIDER THIS

Following are some categories of entry points to consider as you design your presentations. I encourage you to expand this list as you discover additional ways to connect people to musical works.

Potential Entry Points

Musical Elements

- Melody (melodic contour, specific themes and motives, melody vs. accompaniment, scales, modes, embellishment and ornamentation . . .)
- Harmony (parts playing in harmony, major vs. minor, consonance vs. dissonance, tone clusters, diminished chords . . .)
- Counterpoint (contrapuntal forms, imitation, canon, fugue, basso continuo)
- Rhythm (beat, meter, rests, tempo, cross rhythms, subdivision, dotted rhythms, triplets, syncopation, polyrhythms, ostinato, tempo rubato, accelerando . . .)
- Form (binary, ABA, rondo, sonata form, twelve-bar blues, thirty-two-bar song structure, theme and variations . . .)
- Dynamics
- Articulation (legato, staccato, accents . . .)
- Timbre (sound of instruments, special effects, mutes, multiphonics, harmonics, pizzicato, orchestration, Fach, electronic effects . . .)
- Genre and style

Common Metaphors Used to Express Musical Ideas

- Layers (foreground and background, rhythmic layers, instrumental layers)
- Conversation (dialogue, argument, interruption, antecedent-consequent phrase structure)
- Tension and release
- Contrast (instruments, dynamics, articulation, themes . . .)
- Mood (gloomy, peaceful, manic, anxious . . .)
- Emotion (sorrow, joy, anger, disappointment, surprise, love, hate . . .)
- Energy (rhythmic, dynamic, tempo . . .)
- Patterns (melodic, rhythmic, harmonic, formal)
- Texture
- Surprise
- Echoes
- Transformation

Additional Aspects Related to Specific Works

- Narrative or programmatic content (stories, sounds and depictions of nature, poems . . .)
- Characters (e.g., operatic or programmatic works)
- Word-painting
- Style (genre, dance forms, folk influences, national characteristics)
- Biographical or historical context
-
-
-
-

CONSIDER THIS

What kinds of experiences might have opened my sixteen-year-old ears to the greatness of Bartok's music?

- After demonstrating a few of Bartok's stringed instrument "special effects," from String Quartet No. 4, the ensemble could collaborate with the audience to create a one-minute piece that uses these unconventional sounds. Allowing me to explore Bartok's timbres creatively would allow me to perceive them more deeply.
- To introduce Bartok's melodic language, the quartet could teach the audience to sing one of the Hungarian folk songs he collected—one that is melodically and rhythmically related to a movement that follows. Having sung in Bartok's melodic language, I could process his melodies more easily.
- The ensemble could have led the audience in a clapping activity that uses Bartok's rhythmic motives to introduce the concepts of imitation and counterpoint.
- Before hearing String Quartet No. 6, the audience could be led to reflect on their own experiences of alienation or loss. Entering Bartok's emotional mindset would prepare them to be moved more deeply than if they were merely told the biographical context of the work.

✧ PRINCIPLE #2: Go Beyond Information and Engage through Experience

Going back to Jerry's ice-cream-cone metaphor, your goal is to give your audience a hands-on experience of your chosen entry point. This approach differs radically from traditional music appreciation methods, which tend to rely heavily on verbal information.

Information is not a bad thing; it does help people understand *about* musical works. Some listeners, especially adults, are quite hungry for information, and we do well to provide it. However, *unless information is grounded in an actual experience, it seldom helps a listener's ears.*

Consider my Bartok predicament. Would knowing Bela Bartok's birth and death dates help me to hear counterpoint in his quartets? Would a dictionary definition of *counterpoint* really offer any substantial assistance? Would facts about Bartok's life enable my ears to digest chords and timbres that sounded painfully caustic?

If I had been given such information, I may have listened with a little more contextual knowledge. However, this knowledge would not necessarily have affected my musical perception. Informed audience members may feel successful on an intellectual level, but without an experience, their ears remain fundamentally unaltered.

Michael Tilson Thomas conducts the audience during one of the San Francisco Symphony's *Keeping Score* interactive concerts. Photo credit: Terrence McCarthy

Admittedly, this approach is a departure from more conventional ways of doing things, but you can find precedent for it in the work of Leonard Bernstein and other music educators of the twentieth century. Chapter 4 will provide plenty of ideas for creating and executing these kinds of activities.

When you design an audience interaction, give experience priority over information. Information shared after or during an experience is far more likely to be received and remembered.

✄ PRINCIPLE #3: Tap the Competence of Your Audience

You perform for an audience of experts. Your listeners may *think* they're unknowledgeable, unskilled, or in need of musical enlightenment, but you can prove them wrong by taking advantage of capabilities and knowledge they already possess. Every audience member enters the performance space with many skills and abilities—including musical ones—which we can exploit in ways that are relevant to the music that follows.

CONSIDER THIS

With the help of many musicians, I have been compiling a list of "Things Audience Members Can Do." Here are categorized highlights from the list, which will give you an idea of the skills you can tap through your activities.

Things Audience Members Can Do

Ways Audiences Can Produce Sounds

- Sing, hum, whistle . . .
- Make vocal sounds expressing moods, objects, animals
- Play instruments
- Make use of body percussion—snap, clap, stamp . . .
- Make sounds of different timbres and dynamics

Other Musical Capacities

- Keep a steady beat
- Echo call and response patterns
- Harmonize
- Conduct (tempo, meter, dynamics, articulation, cue and cutoff . . .)
- Respond to conducting signals
- Coach musicians on how to play/Make aesthetic choices about how to interpret music
- Compose original melodies, rhythms, and themes/Make compositional choices
- Determine the repertoire or the program order
- Improvise on percussion instruments or with the voice
- Learn and perform melodies and rhythms
- Accompany musicians

- Perform with the musicians
- Perform as a member of a section

Ways Audiences Can Respond to Music

- Stand up and move (dance, jog, or march in place)
- Sway from side to side/Rock back and forth
- Make hand signals or motions
- Express themselves through gestures or pointing
- Listen or watch for something specific
- Analyze, reflect, or discuss something they have heard
- Express observations and interpretations of the music
- Light lighters
- Play "air guitar" and other instruments

Additional Capacities

- Solve puzzles or riddles
- Play games
- Vote
- Volunteer
- Help musicians demonstrate a concept
- Move or dance
- Act in skits
- Make facial expressions
- Work with a partner
- Tell jokes
- Work in a small group
- Converse with a musician or host/ Have a discussion with a neighbor/ Ask and answer questions
- Paint or draw shapes and pictures/ Draw a shape in the air
- Recognize visual or aural patterns
- Write
- Think, visualize, and imagine
- Recall memories and emotions

When we get an audience to sing a theme, clap a rhythmic accompaniment, or make creative and interpretive decisions about music, we put the listeners in our shoes. They become performers and creators in their own rights. They experience the joys and challenges of making music and gain confidence in their abilities to make musical connections.

Application

As an exercise, pick an entry point from the list of entry points (e.g., "ABA form"). Now, look at the "Things Audience Members Can Do" list and design a few activities that would give the audience a hands-on experience of your chosen entry point. For example:

1. Physicalize ABA form through body motions (e.g., run in place/march in place/ run in place).
2. Sing a familiar song in ABA form.
3. Have some volunteers create some ABA patterns by drawing geometric shapes.

Try this with a few entry points. How many different activities can you create?

⚔ PRINCIPLE #4: Address Multiple Intelligences

Although our listeners bring competences into the hall, they do have diverse perceptual abilities and preferences. Some people are kinesthetic learners who best learn by physically doing something. Others are highly verbal and prefer books and written instructions. Still others rely on strong visual and spatial skills to interpret the world around them.

When performing, we have a responsibility to connect with all of our listeners. If our presentation addresses only one perceptual style, we run the risk of neglecting a majority of our audience. One of the surest ways to connect with everyone in our audience is to target different modes of perception. Harvard professor Howard Gardner's groundbreaking multiple intelligence theory provides an excellent guideline for addressing diverse perceptual styles.

In his book *Frames of Mind*, Gardner identified seven distinct "intelligences," which enable people to perceive and process the world. In theory, we all possess each of these capacities, to a greater or a lesser degree. For each intelligence, I provide a short explanation and an example of how it might be engaged during a concert:

Visual/Spatial Intelligence helps us to perceive and process visual information. Televised orchestral broadcasts tap our visual/spatial intelligence through strategic camerawork. By zooming in on instruments at the moment they perform themes or important accompaniments, the camera focuses our listening. In live concerts, we can achieve this same effect through careful use of lighting or by having musicians stand up when they have the theme. Pictures, projected images, and other visual aids can also stimulate our visual/spatial intelligence.

Verbal/Linguistic Intelligence is our ability to acquire, process, and use language and words. Performers often converse and explain, but they should also consider creative ways to tap the audience's verbal/linguistic intelligence. I have seen some performers give brief writing assignments; others have taught song lyrics and chants (or helped audience members to create them). Yet others have encouraged the audience to express musical interpretations by creating metaphors and similes.

Logical/Mathematical Intelligence encompasses our aptitude for logic, numbers, and reasoning, both deductive and inductive. While this intelligence may initially seem less applicable to interactive performance, we can actually use it to exciting effect. Our audiences enjoy solving deductive puzzles, recognizing or composing musical patterns, and so forth. This intelligence also helps listeners to understand musical form and structure.

Bodily/Kinesthetic Intelligence involves physical coordination skills. Any activity that involves movement, dance, or physical action requires bodily/kinesthetic intelligence. Conducting activities can be particularly useful when they incorporate expressive movement and breathing.

Musical/Rhythmic Intelligence encompasses musical creation, performance, and appreciation. Obviously, any kind of performing, composing, or listening activity requires musical intelligence. If we're doing our job right, we'll be engaging this intelligence every step of the way, even as we tap other modes of perception.

Interpersonal Intelligence is our ability to understand, empathize, and communicate with others. In concerts, interpersonal intelligence is most commonly tapped through discussion, but it is also involved in empathetically grasping what a composer or performer is expressing.

Intrapersonal Intelligence is our capacity for introspection, self-knowledge, and self-awareness. This critical capacity helps us to establish personal interpretations and connections to the music. It also enables us to develop a sense of how to listen successfully. Intrapersonal intelligence is tapped by activities that encourage reflection, personal interpretation, or an awareness of how we react to musical passages.

When designing a fully interactive concert, aim to address each intelligence at least once during the course of the event. If a preparatory segment addresses more than one intelligence, it will be more likely to engage the entire audience.

Application

As an exercise, go back to the "Things Audience Members Can Do" list, and identify the intelligence(s) that corresponds (correspond) to each ability (e.g., "clap a rhythm" involves kinesthetic and musical intelligences; "recognize visual or aural patterns" suggests visual/spatial intelligence and logical/mathematical intelligence).

⚹ PRINCIPLE #5: Reflect

While fast-paced presentations can be exciting and desirable, we need to make sure that every piece sinks in. Reflective activities deepen musical experiences and allow them to settle.

One of my favorite places to perform is a public library in Bethpage, Long Island, where there is a series called *Conversations with Music*. At these events, performers spend an hour performing and conversing with the audience, which consists of approximately a hundred retirees who have a passion for music. One of the most rewarding aspects of these events is their highly investigative nature.

After I perform selections, the audience has an opportunity to share its perceptions with one another and with me. We put the music under a collective microscope. With my instrument, I can demonstrate passages that affirm or clarify people's observations and questions.

Often, all I need to do to stimulate the conversation is to ask three simple questions.* To elicit some initial perceptions, I ask, "So what struck you about this piece?" When someone offers an interpretation that begs further exploration (e.g., "It sounded to me like Paganini was trying to be a diva."), I ask, "What about the music makes you say that?" This nonthreatening question leads observers to articulate the specific musical details behind their interpretations. Often their comments address musical subtleties that I might not have addressed in a formal lecture. Finally, to elicit additional responses, I ask, "Did anyone hear anything else?"

Our individual perspectives are enriched by reflecting on our collective responses. By stopping to notice what we perceived, our listening experience becomes more deeply implanted in our memories.

> Reflection is one of the subtle ingredients that can nudge the audience beyond passive entertainment into the deeper realms of personal and aesthetic response.

Reflection is one of the subtle ingredients that can nudge the audience beyond passive entertainment into the deeper realms of personal and aesthetic response. Of course, not every performance situation is conducive to the intimate dialogue possible at Bethpage. However, any performance has ample opportunity to encourage the audience to think introspectively and interpretively.

Some performers prepare their audiences emotionally by asking questions that evoke memories related to the mood of a subsequent piece. Others ask intriguing aesthetic or compositional questions that cause the audience to listen from a composer's perspective (e.g., "If you wanted to write some music that expressed danger, what kind of qualities would you want it to have?").

A successful tactic I have seen applied to audiences of all ages and sizes is to pause for two minutes to have everyone discuss a question with a partner. Ernest Schelling's New York Philharmonic Young People's Concerts from the 1930s gave even children opportunities to write brief responses in a musical journal.

---

*These questions, learned through Lincoln Center Institute training, were adapted from Visual Thinking Strategies (VTS), a method developed by Visual Understanding in Education (VUE) for exploring works of visual art.

Reflection doesn't always have to involve dialogue or writing. Some musicians have asked audience members to share their musical reactions by drawing pictures, striking poses, or making representative gestures and facial expressions.

When you script a concert, be sure to plan reflective moments and activities. Whether used to prepare the audience to hear a piece or to reexamine it, the extra reflective steps can make the musical experience a lasting memory.

✂ PRINCIPLE #6: Project Your Personality in Your Performance

Teaching Artists Eric Booth and Edward Bilous often share the adage, "Eighty percent of what you teach is who you are." For better or for worse, an audience's musical response is deeply affected by its perception of us. If we appear disinterested or dispassionate, the audience has no incentive to receive our performance. On the other hand, our passions and personalities can inspire listeners in ways that recordings and textbooks cannot.

Our passions and personalities can inspire listeners in ways that recordings and textbooks cannot.

Most performers with substantial followings and successful careers have earned them in part because they project their extraordinary personalities when they perform and speak. Leonard Bernstein's charisma and enthusiasm led an entire

Violinist Itzhak Perlman. Photo credit: Akira Kinoshita

generation to appreciate symphonic music. Violinist Itzhak Perlman's warmth and sense of humor charms any audience regardless of its experience with classical music. Top-grossing pop singers offer fans a variety of attractive images that range from the fun and vivacious party animal to the glamour girl or antihero. In each case, the personality of the performer heightens the audience's enthusiasm for the music.

As an interactive performer, your personality will naturally come into play in your concerts. This doesn't mean that you have to act, adopt an unnatural persona, or be as charismatic as Lenny. It does mean that your programs should reflect your own musical interests and passions and that you should be willing to share them. Choose repertoire that excites you. Be willing to share relevant anecdotes or information about yourself. If you're comfortable with yourself and enthusiastic about what you're doing, your audience will be, too.

Designing Your Interactive Concert

Designing an interactive performance takes considerable time and effort at first, but the more you go through the process, the easier it becomes. For a variety of reasons, I encourage you to design concerts collaboratively rather than individually.

Working with like-minded colleagues usually facilitates and enriches the concert planning process, even for solo musicians or people who prefer to work independently. When ensemble members contribute ideas about repertoire and activities, they tend to participate more actively during the actual performance. However, if some members of your group are anxious or reluctant to interact in performance, you may need to assume the leadership in planning and presenting.

Designing an interactive concert encompasses four basic processes, which often overlap: brainstorming the theme and repertoire, designing activities, scripting and rehearsing the concert, and assessing the performance. This sounds basic, and it is. Nevertheless, how you approach each stage can dramatically affect the quality of your final presentation.

Brainstorming the Theme and Repertoire

During the initial planning stages, your goal is to determine your concert's theme and repertoire.

A good interactive concert theme fulfills four basic criteria:

- The theme is intriguing, challenging, or entertaining for both the performers and the audience.
- The theme invites musical exploration, not just demonstration.
- The theme has an emotional or intellectual "bite."
- The theme is musically strong and original.

Rather than elaborate on these qualifications in the abstract, let's examine a few successful themes that met them quite well:

Music Your Parents Would Hate A woodwind quintet put together a program of its favorite contemporary and avant-garde repertoire and designed a presentation suitable for high school audiences. For each piece, they focused on a different musical element that tended to offend or cause a negative audience reaction. Simultaneously, the group highlighted why fans of the piece love it. Students learned how to listen to each piece with the ears of a musician instead of the mind of a music critic. The performances were framed within an ongoing discussion and analysis of popular musical styles, which the students (or their parents) liked or disliked.

Orchestral Survivor! The Fort Wayne, Indiana, Philharmonic has a hip "unplugged" series, which offers interactive performances for an adult audience. At the height of the popularity of CBS television's first season of *Survivor!* miniseries, the orchestra designed a "survivor" concert, complete with totem poles and flaming torches. The various sections the orchestra competed against one another, completed challenges, and campaigned against the other sections while touting their own section's strengths. One by one, the audience voted sections of the orchestra off the stage, until only one section remained to play the concert's finale. (Despite a percussionist's complaint that the violin tribe should be eliminated because they hog all the notes, the strings were the last section standing—by a margin of five votes.)

Any Music You Can Play, the "Legion of Lows" Can Do Better After lamenting that its repertoire consisted almost entirely of transcriptions, a low brass quartet consisting of two euphoniums and two tubas decided to use this quirk to its advantage. With selections ranging from novelty rags to Renaissance chorales and operatic arias, the musicians juxtaposed their performances with live and recorded excerpts of the original versions of each piece. Using the contrast to highlight the beauty, versatility, and strengths of their instruments, the group humorously coaxed the audience to adopt the "low brass chauvinist's worldview."

Was Brahms a Klezmer? A YMHA booked a violin–piano duo to present an interactive recital demonstrating how folk music influenced nineteenth-century composers. Instead of explaining folk elements as they went along, the musicians devised an approach that encouraged the audience to listen analytically.

First, the duo began by performing and defining several different folkdances. Then, without revealing the titles, they performed classical works as the audience listened to determine which folkdance elements were present. For the last segment of the concert, the duo performed various selections, and the audience had to determine whether the musicians were performing a folkdance or a classical composition inspired by one. The inquiry helped to underscore the differences between pure folk music and folk-inspired composition. For theatrical flair, the performers designed their presentation to have the fun, suspenseful feel of a quiz show.

Free at Last A jazz quartet that specialized in the free jazz works of disciples of Ornette Coleman and John Coletrane held a preconcert workshop that explored the questions "What is freedom?" "What are ways people can express or celebrate freedom?" and "How can you express freedom or the struggle for freedom with musical instruments?" Participants used kazoos and percussion to give expression to their own ideas about freedom. During the concert, the musicians continued to explore these questions, and for the grand finale, those who had performed during the workshop joined the musicians onstage to play the final piece.

Each of these concert themes succeeds because it addresses musical issues that are compelling to performer and audience alike. When beginning your planning process, take the time to develop a theme with rich possibilities and interesting implications. A good, highly marketable theme strategically taps the natural curiosity and interests of the audience. It suggests a fun, humorous, or thought-provoking experience. A good theme also is attuned to the natural abilities and personality of your ensemble.

Intriguing themes often revolve around a question. When given the challenge of presenting a school concert about American music, a Manhattan School of Music brass quintet considered the following questions as potential organizing themes: *What makes music sound American? How did the development of American musical styles parallel American history?* and *How does American classical music reflect contemporary American culture?* Each question suggests a rich and specific inquiry that can be explored with much more depth and variety than a generic "Here's some American music" presentation.

Once you have decided your theme, finalize your repertoire. Note the duration of each selection, and consider possible program orders. Do you want your program order to be surprising? cyclical? emotionally shaped? logically structured? Without interaction, would the concert still feel musically satisfying? Usually, it is nice to begin with an attention-grabbing segment and end with a culminating piece that ties all of the elements of your presentation together. Your intervening works should offer a variety of tempos, styles, durations, or moods. Many ensembles have reported that it is helpful to have a slightly longer or more substantial work as an "anchoring work" or "main course."

In general, a "two-thirds music and one-third interaction" formula is ideal. In other words, if you are preparing a forty-five-minute program, you should aim to have about thirty minutes of music and fifteen minutes devoted to preparatory activities, reflection, and questions.

Designing Activities

When you design activities, always begin by investigating each piece in-depth. It is helpful to listen to a work several times, jotting down your impressions from each hearing. First, listen for pleasure and make note of any initial impressions and reactions. Next, pretend to be the typical audience member who will attend your event, and do your best to listen through his or her ears. This step is particularly helpful when preparing presentations for children or nonmusicians. Finally, listen with your analytical perspective as a trained musician—preferably while reading a score. If you are planning a concert as a group, each member can assume one of these roles, and you can share your diverse observations after just one hearing.

Listening from multiple perspectives will help you to describe, analyze, and interpret each work fully. From your observations, it will be relatively easy to generate a list of potential entry points. After brainstorming entry points for all of the works, circle the entry points that best illuminate each work while supporting your concert's theme.

CONSIDER THIS

When searching for the right entry point, some helpful questions to ask are:

- *What makes this work great? What excites me about it?*
- *What do I especially hope my audience notices?*
- *Is there anything unusual, cool, or striking about the work?*
- *Is there any musical element or metaphor that underpins the entire piece?*

- *What entry points would make good aural or visual "hooks" for first-time listeners?*
- *What difficulties would a first-time listener encounter in this work?*
- *Is there anything programmatic or historical about the work that would help a listener?*
- *What aspects of this piece are so strong and immediate that they need no activities to highlight them?*

Application

Useful questions for designing activities around an entry point:

In what ways does this concept manifest itself in my audience's everyday life? How can this concept be experienced

—by a physical activity?
—by a visual aid or a visual activity?
—by singing, making sounds, or playing musical instruments?
—by a dramatic sketch?
—through an analogy or anecdote?

How could the entire audience actively illustrate this concept? one volunteer? a group of volunteers?

Refer to your list of "Things Audience Members Can Do" for additional interactive ideas.

Once you have selected entry points for each work, design activities that will draw the audience into the work via those entry points. Make the activities as hands-on and experiential as possible. Strive for a variety of presentational formats, and address different perceptual styles.

When you choose your entry point, be sure that it really underpins the piece you are performing. Also, make sure that your activity conveys how the entry point functions in the musical work.

Sometimes, musicians lead brilliant activities that sensitize the audience to one spectacular moment, but for the rest of the piece, the listeners are left in the dark. Other times, musicians create generic activities that teach a concept well, but fail to illuminate the music because the activity has not been tailored to the specific work.

One fascinating example that demonstrates both shortcomings comes from a good friend who was conducting a youth orchestra's family concert entitled *Wake Up and Smell the Orchestra: A Concert of Morning Music.*

At the beginning of the concert, a few musicians (a violinist, a flutist, a tuba player, and a triangle player) were to step forward to audition for the distinction of "best musical alarm clock"—a very fun, inquiry-based activity. Much to the tuba player's disappointment, the dress-rehearsal audience ultimately voted that they would prefer to wake up to a triangle.

Next, the orchestra performed the opening of Richard Strauss's *Also Sprach Zarusthustra* (made famous by Stanley Kubrick's film *2001: A Space Odyssey*). At the climax of the opening, the percussionist dutifully entered with Strauss's extended triangle roll.

The triangle roll was a cool moment. Most people commented that they had never consciously noticed it before, and they were grateful to have been led to discover it. The preparatory activity was fun and entertaining. The piece was a great concert-opener. Nevertheless, the conductor was dissatisfied with himself. He felt that in many regards, his presentation had missed the mark:

> The more I listened to people's feedback, the more I realized I was leading them
> in the wrong direction. After all, is Richard Strauss's *Also Sprach Zarusthustra*
> really about a triangle roll? Is that what's so awe-inspiring about it? What
> about the brass fanfare? The pounding timpani solos? The deep pedal tones
> of the bass instruments? Is the literary work that inspired Strauss, Friedrich
> Nietzsche's *Also Sprach Zarusthustra,* a meditation on alarm clocks? No! It's
> about a deeper kind of awakening.

To illumine Strauss's music more fully, the activity was adjusted so that the instrumentalists who auditioned would be those who play important themes in this introduction. Instead of inventing their own "alarm clock sounds," they would audition with Strauss's themes or a similar phrase. (In the case of the brass, the conductor composed and substituted a similar fanfare so that Strauss's instantly recognizable theme would remain a surprise at the performance.)

Instead of voting for which instrument sounded the most like an alarm clock, families in the audience were led to discuss, "If this instrument were an alarm clock, what kind of person or creature would wake up to it?" After sharing suggestions, the conductor complimented the audience on how "awake" their imaginations were. He then related how Strauss was using music to demonstrate Nietzsche's ideas about the awakening of the imagination and the human spirit. During the performance, listeners could notice how all the instruments and themes combined to create a monumental sense of awakening.

And they still noticed the triangle roll.

Scripting and Rehearsing the Concert

As the activities emerge, you may wish to change the order of pieces. Some musicians believe that it is best to end the concert with the most interactive, participatory part to avoid an anticlimax.

Once you have the overall structure finalized, write a script for your concert. The script can range from a succinct one-page outline to an elaborate script with prepared dialogue. If you take the former approach, be thorough and specific; if you take the latter, be sure to allow room for flexibility, spontaneity, and audience response. In most situations, it's best to prepare both a one-page outline and a formally written script. Whatever you do, avoid reading your script during the performance.

When creating your script, plan effective transitions from preparatory activity to performance and from each work to the next. Highlight relationships between the different pieces, and include reflective moments.

Once your script is essentially completed, begin rehearsing. Run the script a few times without the music. The activities and spoken parts of the concert should be given at least as much rehearsal time as the musical parts. Once you are comfortable performing the entire program, hold a dress rehearsal for an audience of your colleagues, your family, or anyone who is available and willing to participate. The dress rehearsal will highlight any rough places that need to be reworked, reworded, or refined. Audio and video recordings of the rehearsal can provide extremely helpful feedback.

Postperformance Assessment

After your performance, take time to assess it. Interview audience members about their experiences. What struck them about the performance? What were their favorite parts and pieces? Written questionnaires (which can be handed out as a program insert and deposited in comment boxes at the exits) can provide extremely helpful feedback, as well as useful quotes for your press kit. If you have hired a videographer, he or she can interview the audience as they leave the performance.

As a group and with colleagues, watch a videotape of your concert. Make observations and comments. Are there any moments that particularly stand out? Which parts engaged the audience the most? Why? What could you do next time to make those successes even deeper or better? What feedback did you receive from the audience after the performance?

Note any adjustments you found yourself making during the performance. What did you learn? If something didn't work out as well as you had planned, determine the reasons. Did the audience need clearer instructions? Did an activity need one or two additional steps in order for it to work?

Find additional venues for performing this program, and start designing your next one!

Engage! Archetypes for Interaction

Now that you understand the underlying principles of interactive concerts, let's examine the fundamental types of audience interaction. Since every interaction is centered on an entry point, let's first consider how we can use entry points most effectively.

How Entry Points Work

Entry points can help people to appreciate musical works in essentially three ways: on a purely musical level, on an intellectual/metaphorical level, or on a personal, emotional level.

For example, a pianist may decide that the driving force behind a Chopin Prelude is the desire for harmonic resolution. Her chosen entry point is consonance and dissonance. A presentation that contrasts the instability of diminished chords with the stability of major and minor triads would address listeners on a purely musical level.

Pianist and composer Beata Moon gives an interactive performance. Photo courtesy of Beata Moon

If this pianist decides to explore consonance and dissonance through the analogy of tension and release, she will connect her listeners in a more metaphorical way. By offering a familiar parallel to the purely musical concept, a sophisticated musical entry point becomes accessible and understandable to a broad audience.

If the presentation involves a step where the listeners identify their own personal stresses and the ways they find relief, the entry point would help the audience to find personal, emotional meaning in the music.

Purely musical use of entry points enables the audience to listen actively like a musician. Intellectual or metaphorical use of entry points helps to universalize and demystify musical concepts. Personal, emotional aspects of entry points allow listeners to establish individual connections with the musical work.

The most comprehensive activities use entry points to connect the audience musically, intellectually, and emotionally.

The earlier pianist could address all three of these dimensions through the following multistep activity:

1. Ask the audience to list common tensions in contemporary life and ways in which people find relief from them. Document the lists on a flipchart.
2. Get the audience to express items on the list by alternately sustaining and relaxing tension in various muscle groups.
3. Repeat the tension-release activity, but this time, accompany it with chords from Chopin's Prelude.
4. Add a vocal element to the exercise by having the audience sing a diminished harmony and its resolution as they tense and release muscles.
5. Introduce and perform the prelude as the audience listens for musical tension and release.

Let's refer back to the revised *Also Sprach Zarusthustra* example from Chapter 3 and see how it addresses all three dimensions of the entry point.

The basic idea behind the interaction was, "How does Richard Strauss use orchestration to convey a sense of spiritual awakening?" On a purely musical level, the entry point was orchestration. The audience was musically introduced to this entry point by hearing Strauss's instruments and themes in isolation. On a more metaphorical level, the audience listened for awakening and character. On a personal level, listeners had the opportunity to form their own individual interpretations of Strauss's orchestrated themes. The activity gave listeners three dimensions for connecting to the music, and they responded with enthusiasm.

Activities do not always need to include more than one way of connecting, but be intentional and strategic about how you are helping listeners to connect. To ensure your chosen entry point has the maximal effect, ask yourself "How do I want the listener to relate to this piece?" "Am I connecting the listener musically?" "Is this abstract musical concept comprehensible?" and "How can I make this music personally relevant?"

Interactive Archetypes and Strategies

There are myriad ways you can interact with your audiences. Following are eighteen of the most common and effective archetypes for engaging your listeners. As you read, notice which strategies you tend to favor, and note new approaches you would like to try. You'll find quite a bit of information and ideas in this section, so take your time. You may find it helpful to revisit this chapter as you study the interactive concert transcripts in Appendix A.

Piece Simulation   In a piece simulation, you and your audience create or perform something analogous to the music they are about to hear. For instance, before performing Heinrich Biber's passacaglia, a piece consisting solely of virtuosic variations over a repeated bass line (G-F-Eb-D), you and your listeners can create your own passacaglia. Simply teach them to sing Biber's bass line and play variations above it.

To prepare listeners for "The Little Hut on Chicken's Legs" from Modest Mussorgsky's *Pictures at an Exhibition*, some musicians have simulated the music by leading a call-and-response rhythmic chant accompanied by clapped accents. The form and rhythms of the chant came directly from Mussorgsky's movement.

The logistics of piece simulations will vary from piece to piece. The primary aim is to get the audience creating and performing something that is as much like the next work as possible. Doing so will cause them to recognize aspects of their performance in the subsequent work. Because a piece simulation is one of the most powerful interactions, try to include one in every concert.

Listening Challenges and Activities   When you set up a piece, it is always helpful to give the audience a clear listening focus or challenge that stems from your entry point. The ideal listening assignments reward listeners in musically or personally significant ways. Counting how many times the bass line repeats in Pachelbel's Canon in D has little personal or musical value. A better approach would help listeners to hear how the lines develop, intensify, and follow one another in canon.

Sometimes, listening can be turned into a physical assignment, activity or game. At a Hudson Valley Philharmonic concert, audience members used hand signals to silently demonstrate their recognition of themes from Tchaikovsky's *Romeo and Juliet Fantasy Overture*. Listeners would put their hands over their hearts or make a fist, according to whether the orchestra was playing love themes or conflict themes. Some conductors teach listeners to conduct along with a piece that has a strong metrical feel or widely contrasting dynamics. (And for a real kick, volunteers can be invited to conduct the orchestra in an encore of the work!)

Improvisation   Improvisation adds an air of excitement to a performance. Even musicians who do not consider themselves improvisers have effectively used improvisational techniques during an interactive concert. Following are a few ways that you can use improvisation:

1. Given a few parameters, volunteers from the audience can come onstage and improvise an instrumental or vocal solo. Usually, your volunteers will need one or two clear parameters (e.g., "Start slow, then get faster

and faster" or "start with low notes, and get higher and higher"). A little practice time also helps volunteers to succeed.

2. Performers can lead an improvisation that involves the whole audience in making music or sound. For instance, in concerts featuring the "Thunderstorm" movement from Beethoven's Symphony No. 6, performers have often led the audience in an improvised "thunderstorm" consisting of snapping, patting, stamping, and vocal sounds that approximate the dynamic shifts of the symphony.

3. Some contemporary pieces include improvised parts for the audience or the musicians. Feel free to commission new ones!

4. Performers can improvise music with one another based on audience suggestions, choices, and parameters. At one concert at the Tanglewood Music Festival, a French horn player and a double bassist improvised a confrontational duet, which represented a battle between a hero and a villain.

5. Improvisation can also take the form of improvised movement, dance, or drama instead of music.

Improvisation provides unique opportunities for you and your audience to experiment with musical concepts and ideas. Exploring an entry point through spontaneous creation gives your audience a clearer picture of how the entry point functions than if you merely demonstrate it. Your audience will also have the satisfaction of participating in musical creation.

Composition   Effective composition activities are tricky within a concert setting, but with a little forethought, they can prove quite successful and musically revealing. Like improvisation, composition gives your audience the opportunity to manipulate musical materials. Composition opens up the creative process and can even result in music that resembles the works you are performing.

In a concert that taught children to listen for musical patterns and musical forms, the musicians of the Bridgehampton Chamber Music Festival helped children to compose. Using voices and a xylophone, listeners created melodies and short pieces in the forms of the pieces to be presented. The audience gained an active sense of how composers put pieces together, how the forms work, and how to *hear* them.

A few keys to making in-concert composition work:

1. Composition is a decision-making process, and an aesthetic one at that. If audiences are making random, unhearing decisions, they are not composing. You need to provide a clear framework for making aesthetic choices. ("So here's the first note of our 'triumphant melody'; do you want the next note to go up or down? Why? How far? Let me play you some options . . . let's vote on which one sounds more triumphant!")

2. In order to make melodic decisions, the audience needs a melodic tool. In addition to responding to a performer's demonstration of compositional choices, audiences can respond to visually structured instruments, such as the Chimalong metallophone, which has multicolored pipes for

distinguishing the various pitches. In effect, the audience can "compose by color." Of course, audiences can also express their melodic urges by humming or singing; the human voice is actually the best melodic tool of all.

If you can actually have a composer on stage to develop the audience's ideas at a piano or another instrument, you can create some really exciting stuff. Commissioned pieces with pre-composed options (to be chosen by the audience at the performance) work well, too.

3. Tailor your parameters to the kind of piece you want. If you want to compose a singable, happy tune, the major pentatonic scale makes a great foundation. If you want to create dance music, choose an appropriate meter and tempo.
4. If you have enough musicians, you can break the audience into small groups and have one musician work with each group to create and interpret a newly composed piece of music.
5. One tactic that is always a hit at a community-based concert is to have people or children from the community compose a piece to be performed at the event. This will take considerable advance work on the part of Teaching Artists, but the payoff is well worth the effort. Helping ordinary people to compose is a whole book unto itself; stay tuned . . .

Audience "Perform-Along"   In this type of activity, the audience has a chance to perform with the musicians as they play. A real perform-along is more sophisticated than simply clapping the beat. Rather, the audience learns a part and performs it in response to visual or musical cues.

The New York Philharmonic has led "sing-alongs" where the audience performs the "Ode to Joy" from Beethoven's Symphony No. 9 with the orchestra. Carnegie Hall's education program has used pre-concert Teaching Artist workshops to prepare audience members to perform vocal and recorder parts in a concert with the Orchestra of St. Luke's.

In lieu of preparatory workshops, simpler accompaniments and parts can be learned during a concert.

One of the major achievements of perform-alongs is that they totally demolish the delineation between listeners and performers. For a moment, audience members enjoy the thrill of being equal partners with great musicians. What more could a music-lover want?

Musician Coaching   The audience can coach performers on everything from mood to tempo to dynamics, and so on. A musician coaching pays the most dividends when tied to a specific, piece-related inquiry.

For instance, during a children's concert focused on "What makes music sound heroic?" a trumpet player performed the fanfare from Rossini's *William Tell Overture* in a completely nonheroic way: he played the solo softly, smoothly, slowly, and in a minor key. The audience offered suggestions for making the solo more heroic until it finally became Rossini's original version. In another instance, an orchestra performed "The Aquarium" from Camille Saint-Saëns *Carnival of the Animals* in a very plain manner and took suggestions from the audience on how to give the music more of a "watery" feeling.

Audience members enjoy making interpretive decisions about how a piece will be performed. Try letting them tinker with dynamics, tempo, and other musical aspects.

Musician Audition   Sometimes in an interactive performance, musicians can audition for a particular improvisational or musical role. At a New York Philharmonic Young People's concert, prior to a performance of Aaron Copland's "Variations on a Shaker Melody" from *Appalachian Spring*, the audience and orchestra created their own original variation on Copland's theme. As part of the process, various instruments auditioned to perform the melody and accompaniment parts.

At a Tanglewood Family Concert, musicians turned an audition into a competition: they tried to see who could sound the most like a bug. The winner had the dubious distinction of being swallowed by a "frog" instrument in an improvisation. The orchestra segued to Rimsky-Korsakov's "Flight of the Bumblebee," and other buggy selections.

Visual Activities/Visual Aids   Because many people are visual learners, it is important to find ways to include visual elements in your interactive performance. Visual aids and props are helpful, but they are most effective when performers use them in active ways that reflect or respond to musical content. At one children's orchestra concert, a huge gray tarpaulin helped people to notice the many varieties of musical waves that Felix Mendelssohn creates in his *Hebrides* overture, which depicts a rolling, stormy sea. Volunteers from the audience came forward and shook the tarpaulin to simulate ocean waves that corresponded to orchestral excerpts demonstrating Mendelssohn's different wave intensities. Watching something analogous to the sounds helped to focus the listeners' ears.

In some circumstances, your audience can draw, paint, or decorate something. One fun activity for baroque musicians is to let artistic volunteers decorate a larger-than-life score before the performance, and then interpret those pictures through ornamentation.

Multimedia   Recently, orchestras and other performing arts organizations have begun to make more use of technology, lighting, and multimedia in concert situations. Concert pianist Bruce Brubaker sometimes makes subtle, innovative use of colored lighting effects in his concerts and recitals, as does the new music chamber orchestra Absolute Ensemble. Carnegie Hall's education programs deserve special recognition for their successful use of listening maps and animated icons to help listeners follow musical themes and forms.* Without a doubt, multimedia has incredible potential, and new possibilities are on the horizon.

---

*Visit www.carnegiehall.org or www.listeningadventures.org for online examples.

The New York Philharmonic features student art in a multimedia approach to Mussorgsky's *Pictures at an Exhibition*. Photo credit: Stephanie Berger

But before we get overexcited and spend vast sums of money on the latest computerized lighting, projection, and animation systems, we should be clear on one thing: *multimedia is beneficial only to the extent it enhances the listening or artistic experience.* Often, in a well-intentioned attempt to dazzle ticket buyers, multimedia efforts end up creating expensive, unnecessary, and unhelpful distractions. In order for multimedia to be effective, it must do something for our ears.

I took my first real plunge into the realm of multimedia when I created a slideshow for the Hudson Valley Philharmonic's performance of Bedrich Smetana's tone poem *Vlatava (The Moldau)*, which depicts a journey from the source of a river to its mouth. As the river flows, it passes hunters, a wedding, a moonlit scene, rapids, a castle, and so forth. The work would be performed twelve times as part of a young people's concert tour for thousands of school children.

As a visual analogue to Smetana's journey, the slideshow took us on a parallel journey from the headwaters of the Hudson River to its mouth in Hudson Bay. For every six seconds of music, I painstakingly chose an appropriate slide to correspond to Smetana's imagery and orchestration.

At the concerts, the elementary and middle school audience listened attentively for the work's duration. However, I noticed that I did not listen to the music in the same way as when there were no images. For better or for worse, visual images do sap quite a bit of our attention. If we aren't careful, multimedia efforts can relegate music to a background role, and listening can become more passive.

Cellist Yo-Yo Ma collaborates with pipa player Wu Man in the New York Philharmonic's *A Silk Road to China* interactive concert. Photo credit: Michael DiVito

I do believe that the slideshow had musical integrity, and according to many teacher evaluations, it helped visually oriented audience members to maintain their focus. However, given our art form's aural nature and our culture's overreliance on visual stimuli, I would not advocate relying exclusively on this kind of approach.

Another danger of multimedia is that it increases one's susceptibility to Murphy's law. At one of the shows, our slide projector mysteriously became unplugged, and we heard Smetana's piece without visuals. I was relieved to notice that the listeners were still able to focus on the music, since the orchestra had demonstrated themes from the different sections beforehand.

Interdisciplinary Approaches Musicians have become increasingly involved in collaborating with choreographers, filmmakers, actors, storytellers, and other artists. Of particular note are Yo-Yo Ma's *Inspired by Bach* interdisciplinary explorations of J. S. Bach's cello suites, which aired on PBS television.

Wendy Law, a graduate of Juilliard's Arts in Education program, recently began to bring interdisciplinary strategies to the recital hall itself. Wendy collaborates with dancers, actors, storytellers, and composers to design evening-length experiences where storytelling, dancing, and audience interactions alternate and coincide with performances of standard cello repertoire. The various art forms complement each other and highlight the mood and structure of the cello music.

The rewards of collaboration are many, and if all artists strive to give the audience entry points into one another's artworks, amazing and aesthetic experiences will follow. The Gogmagogs, an ensemble founded in 1995 by theater director Lucy Bailey and violinist Nell Catchpole, has worked with composers and choreographers to create serious, theatrical musical performances where the musicians move and act while playing their instruments. Their interdisciplinary approach has resulted in a new genre of musical performance with its own steadily growing repertoire. Other companies such as Vision into Art, founded by composers Nora Kroll-Rosenbaum and Paola Balsamo Prestini, are following suit by developing interdisciplinary creations involving art, dance, music, poetry, and film.

Of course, it is possible to include an interdisciplinary approach for just one piece or segment of a concert as well. As with multimedia, keep an eye out for maintaining musical integrity. Constantly ask yourself, "Does this serve the music? Does this enhance the hearing of this piece?" or "Is this a satisfying work of art unto itself?"

Using One Performance as a "Warm-Up" for the Next Work   Sometimes one musical performance can sharpen the listeners' perceptions of a work that follows. A televised Boston Pops concert presented an extraordinary example of this approach. Prior to a performance of a movement from Igor Stravinsky's *The Rite of Spring*, two guest musicians from the Broadway musical *Stomp!* were invited to the stage.

Dressed in garbage can lids and other household objects, the guest artists performed a stunning, polyrhythmic percussion duet that was as gymnastic as it was musical. Striking themselves and each other, they built their performance to a thrillingly complex, cacophonous climax. The duet sensitized listeners to rhythm, accents, and sheer unbridled energy. When the orchestra segued to Stravinsky's dance, any listener would hear the raw, visceral, rhythmic power like never before. The guys from *Stomp!* had tweaked our awareness to receive the full impact and vitality of Stravinsky's shocking and invigorating music.

Offering the Audience a Second Helping   Most musicians agree that multiple hearings facilitate deeper understanding of musical works. I am grateful for a recital in which the Muir String Quartet performed Anton Webern's *Six Bagatelles* both before and after intermission. The first hearing familiarized me with Webern's delicate timbres and surprising economy of form; the second hearing allowed me to concentrate more fully on Webern's motives and phrasing.

Second hearings are most helpful for illuminating sophisticated pieces. Any piece that does not reveal all of its treasures on one hearing makes a good candidate for a repeat performance. By offering multiple hearings, you can give the audience the opportunity to listen to a particular piece in different ways.

In interactive performances, we can provide strategic opportunities for the audience to hear works more than once. I once began a family concert with the musicians entering and performing the opening Allegro from a harpsichord concerto by J. S. Bach. After performing other works and leading several activities that heightened the audience's sense of counterpoint and phrase structure, the musicians repeated the Allegro as their finale. The audience was hearing in such a focused way that some listeners said it almost sounded like a different piece. In actuality, the first performance helped listeners to digest the "big picture" of the movement. The intervening activities prepared listeners to notice the details.

Dialogue-Based Activities   Speaking is probably the most common form of interaction between musicians and their audiences. We should
always look for ways to open up the dialogue further. Some
musicians are fond of going out into their audiences to interview people or converse with them. If you have a philosophical
question to pose to the audience, you can take a few minutes
to have the audience "talk among themselves" and then share
their conclusions with the large group. When using dialogue,
keep it creative, and give the audience input when you can.

Speaking is probably
the most common form
of interaction between
musicians and their audi-
ences. We should always
look for ways to open up
the dialogue further.

The contemporary music group Eighth Blackbird sometimes structures its
dialogues in ways that illumine the work it is about to perform. For instance, a
rondo movement might be preceded by a spoken introduction in rondo form.

Demonstration   While not necessarily interactive in and of itself, demonstrating musical ideas and themes can be enormously helpful to listeners. Usually,
a savvy performer can find ways to enhance the demonstration through audience participation. If audiences can perform or manipulate the material being
demonstrated, they will be even more likely to recognize it when they listen to
the performance.

An audience can usually be taught a melody or a rhythm through a call-and-
response process. When teaching melodies and rhythms, adding physical gestures
to the singing (such as tracing the highs and lows of melodic contours with the
hands) can prove helpful to kinesthetic and visual learners. Sometimes examples
are perceived more clearly if the demonstration initially happens slower than the
performance tempo.

Keep all demonstrations concise, yet substantial enough to be processed and
remembered.

Contextual/Metaphorical   Oftentimes, metaphors or contextual information
about a composition can provide effective entry points, particularly with programmatic music. In these cases, you can design an activity that invokes the metaphor or information.

For example, "Limoges" from Modest Mussorgsky's *Pictures at an Exhibition* is a movement inspired by a painting of women gossiping at a French marketplace. In his manuscript, Mussorgsky actually wrote down three silly rumors,
which he thought the ladies might have been sharing:

- Big news! M. de Puissangeout has just recovered his runaway cow.
- Mme. de Remboursac has got wonderful porcelain dentures.
- M. de Panta-Pantaléon is still inconvenienced by his nose, which is as
  red as a peony.

In the orchestral version of this movement, instruments depict the women's
chattering and by repeating brief musical ideas and passing them back and forth,
sometimes with slight modifications—quite like real gossip!

In concerts, a few volunteers can come forward to play the children's gossip
game "Telephone" with simplified versions of Mussorgsky's rumors. Once the

listeners are lined up, a musician whispers one rumor to be passed on down the line. The last person reports the rumor (possibly altered) to the audience.

Not only does this activity bring out a bit of contextual information about the piece, but the repetition and distortion of the gossip have clear musical analogues, which can be demonstrated prior to performing the movement.

Games   In the previous example, a children's game provided a fun way to illumine the music. In another instance, a string quintet from the Manhattan School of Music used "musical charades" to put a puzzle-solving spin on Camille Saint-Saëns *Carnival of the Animals*. Listeners had to use musical clues to determine what animal the different instruments were depicting.

The New York Philharmonic Teaching Artist Ensemble invoked *Sesame Street*'s "One of these things is not like the others" game to highlight how one instrument plays in a totally different key in a dance from Igor Stravinsky's *Petrouchka*. "Simon Says," "Follow the Leader" "20 Questions," "Truth or Dare," and other games can easily be exploited in concerts for children, as well as for adults. Make a list of fun games, and keep it handy.

Puzzles or Problems to Solve   Everybody likes mysteries, riddles, and puzzles. One group of Manhattan School of Music students created an educational concert with a *Mission Impossible* theme. Each musician would portray a secret agent who would be given a paper with a secret mission or mystery to solve. The audience helped each agent with his or her assignment. Listeners learned musical concepts through problem solving and discovery instead of didactic explanations. Of course, having each message self-destruct with the help of combustible flash-paper didn't hurt the entertainment value of their presentation!

Other   This list of activity types is by no means comprehensive! Continue to observe and categorize activities, and create new ways to connect to your audience. Be sure to share them with the rest of us!

Application

Choose a work or two that you or your ensemble are performing in concert. Go through the interactive archetypes and design a few different activities that could be used in a concert setting. Try them out. Which seems to be most effective in focusing the audience on the music?

Presenting

The instant we interact with an audience, we enter the theatrical realm. Surprised? I was.

Because I learned about music from lectures, lessons, and master classes, my role models for presenting music were professors and teachers. The minute I stepped into a middle school auditorium, I suddenly realized that gifted presenters rely on much more than a thorough knowledge of their subject matter. I became acutely aware that the most engaging speakers possess a wonderful sense of theatricality and drama, as well as a capacity to receive verbal and nonverbal feedback from their audiences.

Our objective is not to win an Oscar or a Tony, but we should strive to make our events theatrically engaging.

Obviously, our objective is not to win an Oscar or a Tony, but we should strive to make our events theatrically engaging. Our decisions about venue, set, lighting, blocking (stage movement), props, and speaking should incline an audience to stay with the music and work harder as listeners.

As musicians, we forget how the standard concert setup can strike people as inherently boring or alienating. Think about it—a bunch of people in formal wear sit on a stage and play instruments for approximately ninety minutes, then they leave. Such a presentation could appeal only to someone who is an avid listener. Since our primary objective in interactive performance is to help people become successful listeners, we may want to replace unhelpful conventions with more engaging alternatives.

To this end, one of the first things we should consider is our venue. Our choice of performance space can really set the tone for the event. If you are planning a fully interactive concert with considerable audience participation, a large concert hall may not be the most conducive environment.

Adopt a broad view of what constitutes a performance space. You really can play anywhere you like. Serious musical performances have been given at art galleries, factories, golf courses, train stations, supermarkets, church fellowship halls, apartment building rooftops, fitness centers and gyms, boys' and girls' clubs, nightclubs, town squares, children's museums, prisons, music shops, barns, comedy clubs, furniture stores, retirement homes, bookstores, backyards, hotel ballrooms, psychiatric wards, country clubs, hospitals, orphanages, libraries, firehouses, national parks, and other great places. Oftentimes, you can partner with a business or organization that will provide space, sponsorship, discount catering, or other services in exchange for advertising and the customer-drawing power of your presence.

Newband performing in the 2005 production of *Oedipus* by Harry Partch at Montclair State University's Alexander Kasser Theater. Photo credit: Mike Peters

Whatever your venue, consider ways in which you can use and set the space in inviting and provocative ways. I once attended a concert by the microtonal ensemble Newband, which was performing in a small stone cathedral in Brooklyn. Upon entering the church, people encountered a dark sanctuary, save for a blue-lit menagerie of bizarre-looking instruments built by American composer Harry Partch. Giant-sized marimbas, kitharas resembling ancient Greek altars, and glass domes suspended like jellyfish from chains created an expectation of something ancient, contemporary, dramatic, and extraordinary.

The ensemble itself demonstrated a substantial amount of theatrical savvy. Wearing austere, mostly black attire, the musicians solemnly proceeded down the aisle in pairs. Once onstage, they judiciously avoided dark or unlit spaces and remained in light. When performing, they "cheated to the audience" by keeping their bodies and faces turned toward us, even when looking sideways or turning pages. Consequently, it felt like they were always directing all of their energy and music toward us. When performers assumed the occasional speaking or singing role, their steady, varied eye contact made the whole audience feel acknowledged.

At intermission, the house lights went up, and the audience was invited to walk around the performance space to take a closer look at Partch's magnificent contraptions. A stage diagram and instrument guide in the program gave the name, materials, and history of each instrument.

When the house dimmed again, the blue lighting gels had been switched to amber ones to give the impression of natural sunlight. To our surprise, instead of another procession or a conventional entrance from backstage, the performers ambled in from all areas of the church. Dressed like down-and-out itinerants from John Steinbeck's *The Grapes of Wrath* and wearing makeup that gave the appearance of dirt, grease smears, and five o'clock shadows, they hobbled up to us and hoarsely whispered, "Spare a dime, mister? . . . Spare change, ma'am?" Gradually finding their way to their instruments, they commenced Partch's *U.S. Highball*, an epic operatic chronicle of American hobo life during the Great Depression. Remarkably, the instrumentalists who had looked so contemporary and angular before continued to play with intensity and precision while projecting the loose, lazy, and sardonic body language appropriate for Partch's libretto.

Had Newband omitted its numerous theatrical touches, the evening still would have been a musically satisfying concert. However, the ensemble's careful planning and attention to matters of set, lighting, staging, body language, dress, speech, and presentation made the event an electrifying experience I can vividly recall over a decade later.

We need to be just as aware of these presentational aspects when planning our own concerts. For theatrical elements to be effective in a concert, they must be intentional and professional. While some musicians have a natural theatrical flair, anyone can benefit from the insight of a drama coach or producer. For years, Concert Artists Guild has hired Janet Bookspan, a stage director, drama coach, actress, and musician, to groom its competition winners for its community

CONSIDER THIS

The following checklist of questions can help to stimulate theatrical thinking as you plan the presentational aspects of your performance.

- *How could we set the stage in evocative or inviting ways that relate to our theme? How could we use lighting to enhance the concert?*
- *What props might we use?*
- *What kind of dress do we want? If we were to use costumes, what might we wear?*
- *At what points can we make creative entrances or exits? When might we go out into the audience?*
- *What is our plan for moving about onstage? How can we make use of the whole stage? Are there instances where the musicians*

could move while they are performing?
- *What kind of language do we want to use? (formal, informal, bilingual, Shakespearean, etc.) What manner of speaking is best suited to our audience and our theme?*
- *Are there points in our program where we might include actors, dancers, poets, or other kinds of artists?*
- *What can the musicians or ensemble do to enhance their stage presence?*
- *How can we achieve dramatic effects with the musical selections? Can we have the music begin suddenly or in unexpected ways? Could we put performers in the house?*

concerts. Expert input can significantly increase confidence and presentational quality, so seriously consider contacting a professional coach or producer.

Even with professional guidance, we would do well to increase our awareness of two key areas of our presentation: speech and movement.

Speaking

As with performing a musical composition, it's not necessarily what you say, it's how you say it. We all know that we should project from our diaphragms and speak clearly, evenly, and with appropriate spirit. We know not to mumble, rush our words, look at our feet or the ceiling, and we know that reading our lines from a script usually makes for an awkward presentation. In addition to those familiar shortcomings, I have observed two other subtler gaffes to avoid.

As with performing a musical composition, it's not necessarily what you say, it's how you say it.

Sometimes, musicians inadvertently turn their backs to their audience while speaking, and the audience misses the last part of what is being said. Seems odd? It usually happens when musicians are getting ready to play the next piece. In an effort to keep things moving, they move to get their instruments while they are finishing a spoken introduction. To avoid showing the audience your backside, simply finish what you have to say and take the necessary five seconds to get your instrument and your bearings. The audience has a much shorter wait than it feels like onstage.

At the same time, we should avoid being overly formulaic about providing a spoken setup and then having the musicians get ready and begin. There is good theatrical impact when music comes in dramatically, surprisingly, or in conjunction with verbal pauses.

The second common oversight results when musicians start speaking before the applause has died away. As a result, the first sentence or so is unintelligible. Again, this impulse usually comes from a healthy urge to keep the momentum going.

Wait until the applause totally dies down. If you are concerned about people losing focus during a lengthy ovation, you can gently give the audience a cut-off signal, or you can simply ask that applause be withheld until the program's conclusion.

In addition to avoiding detrimental habits, we can consciously use some effective speaking strategies. A positive technique to add to your verbal kit-bag is "ping-ponging." When sharing the stage with other speakers, take turns frequently—even within a paragraph. Changing speakers holds the audience's attention, and they are less prone to "space out" during verbal sections of your presentation. What works for morning television news also works for the stage.

Economize your words. One clear image is worth paragraphs of description; effective metaphors and questions are golden. Include humor where appropriate and effective.

Economize your words.

Also consider how you plan to use silence in your performance. In addition to moments where silence may have a theatrical impact, silence can set up a discipline for listening to music.

Movement and Stage Presence

Again, we know that we shouldn't pace, fidget, gesture excessively, or be a stiff. Nevertheless, we all have habits and mannerisms, good and bad. Watch a video of one of your interactive performances. Give yourself due credit, as well as critique. Document what you learn, and set presentational goals for your next performance.

Aside from monitoring and refining your own habits, start thinking of how you can add theatrical class to your presentations. Look for creative ways to use or enhance the performance space. Consider going into the house during the performance or making an unusual entrance or exit.* Be aware of your light, body position, and eye contact with the audience. No matter what repertoire you are performing, the audience always appreciates a good show.

Also remember that every moment you are onstage, you are a presence on the stage. If you are performing, perform passionately. If you are sitting as another musician speaks or presents, give him or her your attention and focus. This will help the audience to focus.

If you are hosting, but not playing, what you do when the musicians perform can still have a major impact on the audience. When Jon Deak, Associate Principal Double Bass of the New York Philharmonic, hosts a Young People's Concert, he listens in ways that guide the listeners.

Jon Deak hosting a New York Philharmonic Young People's Concert. Photo credit: Michael DiVito

---

*World-class percussion soloist Evelyn Glennie wins the prize for "most theatrical entrance" for entering through the back of Avery Fisher Hall, chanting electronically manipulated alien vocal sounds, bowing an ethereal-sounding instrument called a waterphone, and wearing a silver spandex spacesuit when performing Michael Daugherty's *U.F.O.* with the New York Philharmonic.

His head punctuates the rhythms we hear; his body leans toward the instruments with the primary line; his facial expressions respond to mood of the music. Jon is not following a choreographed routine; he is responding naturally to the music he hears. But he communicates his listening experience in such clear and visual ways that the audience can't help but respond sympathetically.

When you have the role of listening host, think about how you can model listening for your audience. Position yourself in a way that doesn't distract. Some musicians prefer to listen from the side of the stage; others take a slightly off-center or below-the-stage position. If you are in clear view, try adjusting your chair or stool so that your body is at an angle to the musicians and the audience. This way, you can alternately turn your focus toward the musicians or the listeners.

Take the time to plan and polish the presentational parts of your performance. You will gain confidence and finesse, and your audience will notice.

Avoiding Ten Common Pitfalls

So far, we've discussed how to use interactive performance strategies to enliven and deepen an audience's concert experience. In theory, we know what to do. Now, let's learn what not to do!

The following pitfalls appear again and again in my field observations, coaching sessions, and even my own concert-planning process. Unfortunately, these tendencies tend to reappear whenever we begin a new program because we are bucking bad habits, long traditions, and entrenched ways of thinking. The good news is, each of these shortcomings can be avoided or corrected with a little conscientious awareness and a good dose of musical integrity.

✼ PITFALL #1: Words, Words, and More Words . . .

"You're talking a lot, but you're not saying anything!"
—David Byrne, "Psycho Killer"

When audience members describe unsatisfying interactive performances, the most common complaints are "The performers just rambled on and on," or "The language was really technical and hard to understand."

Both of these errors can be avoided in the scripting phase.

The very act of scriptwriting focuses our speech by refining and limiting our words. Even so, our rough drafts will likely have sections that are too long or too verbose. When revising a first draft, try giving yourself the objective of reducing the total number of words by one-third. Look for sections that seem wordy and investigate them. Are you saying only what is necessary? Are you clear and focused in how you say it? Does this spoken section need to be broken up with illustrative musical examples or participatory moments? Speaking the text aloud or reading it to a friend helps tremendously. Occasionally, I even let a computer's voice synthesis software read my text. If the script makes sense when read by a monotonous computer, it's in good shape!

Once the script is concise and eloquent, it's time to check for unnecessary or unexplained technical information and jargon. Although we can do the troubleshooting ourselves, it's helpful to hand the script over to a nonmusician. An objective reader can easily tell when we are speaking a "foreign language" or making little sense about complicated matters.

For fun, see if you can minimize or eliminate speaking components altogether. The first time I designed an interactive concert, my advising professor Dr. Edward Bilous challenged my group to create an audience-participatory concert that had absolutely no speaking until the postperformance reflection. The task seemed impossible and even crazy at first, but we met the challenge through creative improvisations; nonverbal communication; the incorporation of a goofy, clowning character; and a few posters. We were amazed by how deeply musicians could interact without saying a word.

⚔ PITFALL #2: The Interaction Consists Mostly of Analysis and Demonstration Rather Than Exploration and Discovery

Have you ever heard people complain how an English teacher ruined a poem by analyzing it to death? The problem is not that literary analysis is harmful; rather, we become disenchanted because an outside expert has spoiled our opportunity to explore the poem for ourselves. In a similar vein, concerts that rely mostly on passive demonstrations often defeat their purpose by "telling all" in a way that sucks the life out of a piece.

Surprisingly many performances are one or two interactive steps shy of a mind-blowing experience. I recently saw a concert that had a solid theme, coherent script, and wonderful programming. The conductor and narrator presented the music with clarity and enthusiasm. They even articulated a specific listening focus for every work on the program. However, because everything was done in a presentational rather than a participatory fashion, the audience was not as musically engaged or enthusiastic as they might have been. Because we had no hands-on experiences of the entry points, we became passive listeners who (at most) heard only what we were told to hear.

One Juilliard student string quartet's experience demonstrates how inquiry-based discovery proves much more effective than passive demonstration. The quartet was preparing to give an interactive performance of George Crumb's *Black Angels: Thirteen Images from the Dark Land*, an intense modern work for amplified string quartet.

Before performing the third movement, the group was planning to demonstrate the unusual sounds that Crumb obtains by asking the performers to play their instruments with glass rods, thimbles, and paper clips. To complete Crumb's exotic and evocative sonic palate, some musicians would also bow tam-tams (gongs) and water-filled crystal goblets. These combined techniques fill the air with eerie, unexpected, and other-worldly textures.

At the dress rehearsal, the group meticulously demonstrated all of Crumb's sounds. The demonstrations were clear and concise, but somehow, when the movement was finally played, the unusual techniques lost their edge. Ironically, the audience knew what was coming *too* well, so the music no longer surprised or excited us. The quartet realized it had to roll up its sleeves and find a way to familiarize the audience with the objects and their potential timbres, without spoiling Crumb's intrigue.

The group devised a new, inquiry-based strategy that allowed the audience to experiment with the unusual objects. Each quartet member would hold up one of the objects and let the audience give suggestions on how the item might be used to make "sounds from a dark land" with or without his or her instrument. Instead of being passive recipients of information, the audience members would now be wearing George Crumb's shoes as an expressive sound-explorer.

At the concert, listeners were fascinated as each performer tried out the suggestions, many of which proved humorous and challenging. Following this experiment, the audience was primed for the quartet's listening challenge: "Now let's see and hear how George Crumb creates dark sounds and images with these items!"

This time as the group performed, Crumb's effects revealed themselves in the moment. Audience members were pleased to recognize many of their own techniques, but they were also surprised by novel ideas they had not considered.

The quality of the quartet's performance was just as fine in the dress rehearsal, but this time, the audience's experience was vastly different. Why? People were now listening with the mind-set "What happens next?" instead of "We already know what happens next." The dress-rehearsal audience listened as knowledgeable, but passive individuals. The final performance audience listened as Crumb's sound-exploring colleagues, who understood his delight in creating weird sounds with unusual objects.

⚔ PITFALL #3: The Presentational Portions of the Concert Are Underrehearsed

Sadly, many otherwise brilliant concerts suffer from verbal stumbling, delayed responses to spoken cues, or onstage confusion about what comes next. In most cases, the performances could have achieved their full potential with an extra run-through and a few additional hours of oral rehearsal.

As performers, we dedicate thousands of hours of our lives to practicing our instruments and perfecting the music we perform. We naturally hold ourselves to high performance standards. Our dedication to our craft is laudable, but we often forget that the audience holds us to presentational standards that are equally high.

> Rehearse your script more than you think is necessary. . . . I have never seen a concert where the presentational part seemed "overprepared."

Rehearse your script more than you think is necessary. Strive for tight cuing, excitingly crisp back-and-forth between words and music, clarity of focus, and a sense of precision throughout the performance. If there are technical details like lighting or miking, rehearse those aspects as well. I have never seen a concert where the presentational part seemed "overprepared."

During the dress rehearsal of a program by a string orchestra from the Manhattan School of Music's elite Orchestral Performance Program, Mark, a bass player, paused and said: "You know, this movement wasn't quite together. I feel like we really need to spend the rest of our rehearsal time going over the music."

As the group's coach, the last thing I wanted to do was discourage musical rehearsal, but time and again, I had seen excellent musicianship undermined by a sloppy or inadequate presentation.

"Mark, I appreciate your impulse to make the concert as musically solid as possible, but I have to tell you that the performance you just gave would knock the socks off any fourth grader in New York City. However, if you fumble your words, the group won't command the respect and attention it deserves. Every day, those fourth graders watch polished actors and speakers on TV, and like it or not, *that's* the standard they'll apply to your spoken dialogue. Unless you think the group's speaking is ready to hold its own against Hollywood's best, I think we should keep working on presentation."

After a thoughtful pause, Mark and the others agreed. For the record, the group scheduled an additional rehearsal to refine the music and run the script one more time. At the concert, the audience was rapt.

✕ PITFALL #4: The Musical Portion Is Underrehearsed Because the Concert Is Not Perceived as a Significant Artistic Event

Although we musicians usually hold ourselves to high performance standards, we sometimes make embarrassing mistakes or perform sloppily because we have not adequately rehearsed the music for an interactive event.

Why do we fall short of our usual standards? The reason generally boils down to one of two fundamental issues:

- Organizations are unwilling or unable to compensate us for the necessary rehearsal time, so we give priority to more profitable or higher profile endeavors.
- We or our organizations have a philosophically flawed view of where interactive concerts fit into the scheme of importance.

What do I mean by a philosophically flawed view? Like the rest of the world, today's music scene still suffers from an unspoken hierarchy where the significance of a performance or a performer is based on earnings, fame, venue, and publicity.

A few decades ago, when organizations and individuals concluded that musicians should present their music to communities, schools, and underserved populations (because "it's a nice thing to do; there's grant money for it, and musicians need to develop future audiences"), the added performances were perceived as something extra, or something that musicians had to do, like it or not. Outreach performances became regarded in the same light as spinach: healthful, but not necessarily tasty.

Some performers even regarded interactive performance as work that musicians do until they become professionally established enough that they don't have to bother with it anymore. Conductors and musical directors reinforced this pattern by delegating orchestral outreach concerts to their assistant conductors. (In many cases, this was just as well!)

Categorizing performances as "those that matter much" and "those that matter less" is a flawed and artless approach to music making. People attend concerts because they expect to receive and appreciate the performers' gifts. Offering them anything less than our finest work is simply selfish and rude.

Believe it or not, an untrained audience *can* sense the difference between a good performance and a great one. Listeners may not be able to articulate the difference, but they definitely know and appreciate when performers deliver their absolute best. They also can tell the difference between a performance that the musicians are genuinely delighted to give, and one in which the players are going through the motions with a smile on their faces (or not).

More than likely, you will have at least one pair of highly discriminating ears in every audience. Once after a very low-profile performance, a listener shook my hand and exclaimed, "That was great!" A mutual friend introduced him as international violin soloist and recording artist Gil Shaham. I'm glad I was on my toes that day.

Whenever we walk off the stage, we should feel like we've given our best effort, no matter who's listening or whether or not we are paid. Since you're taking the time to read this chapter, I'm sure you feel the same. Encourage those who don't to change their minds.

Enough said.

❌ PITFALL #5: The Concert Has a Nonmusical Purpose

When I was in fifth grade, two uniformed police officers came to my school and proceeded to show the most horrifying film I had ever seen. The hour-long movie was real footage of heroin addicts shooting up in grungy back-alleys; emergency room workers shoving tubes up the noses of unconscious overdose patients; and screaming, sobbing, chemically altered people whose pained ravings made no sense. I spent the majority of the hour looking at my shoes, feeling queasy, and wondering if anyone was going to barf as had happened when my sister's class had seen this notorious film. I made a mental note to avoid any activities that could lead to a cameo in a police department documentary.

Twenty years later, I am watching a jazz combo play a concert at a middle school. The ensemble is making a futile attempt to convey the same antidrug message as the police film, but unfortunately, their music seems a bit of a non-sequitur. Moreover, the message lacks the effectiveness and authority of professional drug prevention programs—nobody barfs.

The next day, I watch a string quartet attempt to use works by Mozart, Ravel, and Tchaikovsky to teach third graders about the solar system. It's never quite clear what their music has to do with space, but we take a whirlwind tour of the galaxy anyway. Afterward, I can't remember a single fact from the planetary trivia that was hurriedly recited before each excerpt, and the kids I interview don't seem to know what a cello is.

In all fairness, both of these ensembles were merely doing the job they were asked to do. The problem lies in the agenda they were handed.

Confusing, nonmusical programs result when arts organizations try to market their ensembles to schools and communities who are requesting or demanding curricular links or specific ideological messages.

I'm all for designing programs that appeal to the needs of schools and communities, but in the rush for relevance, two crucial principles are often forgotten:

- We musicians are experts on music. It's what we know and do best.
- The experts on drug prevention, literacy, science, math, social work, and so forth specialize in those subjects; it's what they do best.

When music becomes a mere vehicle for a nonmusical agenda, both the musical presentation and the message suffer. If school administrations don't expect the police officers to burst out singing polyphonic antidrug madrigals, why do schools and arts organizations insist that musicians make their programs serve intrinsically unmusical purposes?

> When music becomes a mere vehicle for a nonmusical agenda, both the musical presentation and the message suffer.

Music has merit in and of itself, and any concert of value must ground itself in musical experience. When we depart from the music, we depart from what we know and do best. We cannot be expected to teach other subjects as effectively as our counterparts in those disciplines. When musical substance takes the back burner, we no longer enjoy ourselves and neither does our audience.

Realistically, though, we may have to grapple with the fact that School X won't book any program that doesn't meet State Literacy Standard 2.9. So be it. Find a way to meet that demand with musical integrity.

With a little creativity, you will discover ways to satisfy your client's agenda while maintaining your musical integrity. Here's a crucial hint: you will have the most success if your extramusical agenda provides a metaphor with clear musical manifestations. At the Hudson Valley Philharmonic one year, we created a concert that addressed the demand for a program addressing conflict resolution by exploring how composers expressed conflict and resolution in music.

CONSIDER THIS

If you find yourself under pressure to address nonmusical agendas with your concert, consider the following advice:

1. Begin with music—real music that you want to play. Think of more pieces than you could put on any one concert.
2. Look at your list and ask yourself, "What are some natural connections that could be made to meet the demands of my clients? What is a theme that could have musical meaning as well as extramusical relevance?" If possible, involve a friend who understands your client's perspective. A nonmusician may see the connections more quickly and easily than you can.
3. Once you've found a thematic way to connect your repertoire to the client's demands, brainstorm entry points and design activities that meet the extramusical agenda while heightening the perception of your music.

It can be done. Who knows? Maybe you will be the one who finally creates an effective, musically illuminating drug-prevention show.

✖ PITFALL #6: The Interactive Elements Have Nothing to Do with the Music

Sometimes performers and presenters think of fun, cool ideas that have no apparent connection to the repertoire that is being performed. This brings us to an important principle about our presentations: *If you don't hear a musical connection, your audience won't either.*

I once saw a highly engaging, entertaining orchestra concert on PBS. The conductor's brilliant presentation and interaction led to some stunning insights into sophisticated musical works.

What does "doing the wave" have to do with Felix Mendelssohn's
Italian Symphony? © Creatas/PunchStock

Then, for no apparent reason, he introduced a comedic juggling troupe, which performed its humorous shtick while the orchestra performed a—while the orchestra performed . . . Funny, I have no recollection what the orchestra actually played. Whatever the musical selection was, it became wallpaper for an amusing act that did nothing for our ears or the orchestra.

I do have a happy example of an instance where a particularly savvy performer used a seemingly irrelevant activity to elicit serious musical insights:

Midway through a New York Philharmonic School Day Concert, conductor Bobby McFerrin decided to have a "seventh-inning stretch." Just for fun, McFerrin asked the teenage audience to "do the wave" like people do at baseball games. McFerrin made the incongruous activity all the more humorous by sending the wave from the back of the hall up through the members of the orchestra.

To bring us back from Yankee Stadium to Avery Fisher Hall, McFerrin asked the audience, "What does 'the wave' have to do with the second movement of Mendelssohn's Italian Symphony? Anybody? How was the music we just played like doing 'the wave'?"

After a reflective pause, audience members began to articulate connections:

"The musicians passed themes from one instrument to the other."
"The music was flowing."
"There were waves of dynamics where it'd grow loud and then get soft."

After collecting several cogent observations, McFerrin affirmed them by saying, "Good! Now listen for all those things as we play the third and fourth movements."

Thanks to McFerrin's impulse to make a connection to the music, his seventh-inning stretch did more than refresh our bodies: It sensitized us to the "waves" in the music that followed.

✕ PITFALL #7: The Interactions Lack Variety

Sometimes a concert's interactions are completely relevant to the music, but they all amount to essentially the same activity. When audience interactions lack variety, participation becomes a tiresome chore.

This pitfall surfaced at an otherwise pleasant family concert performance by a husband and wife folk duo. Both of them sang and performed skillfully on autoharp, guitar, harmonica, and fiddle. Their repertoire offered a nice variety of tempi, emotions, and cultural origins. Their set was organized, well paced, and thoughtfully programmed.

The couple occasionally asked the audience to chime in during a song. Three of the opportunities involved randomly making animal sounds on cue; others involved filling in lyrical blanks. While most of the audience enjoyed the first interaction (making a chicken-clucking cacophony on cue), by about the third animal-sound song, even the youngest children lost their enthusiasm for playing along.

Why? The interactive strategy was one-dimensional and not particularly musical. The novelty of participation gave way to predictability and pointlessness.

CONSIDER THIS

What could the folk duo have done to create activity variety? Here are a few possible approaches that would have deepened the interactions and engaged the audience in more ways.

- The audience could learn to sing the chorus of one song so that the participation would be musically grounded. The whole concert could conclude with an audience sing-along that involves everyone.
- The audience could create and perform a rhythmic accompaniment to a song. This process could be used to highlight how one member of the duo always provided accompaniment while the other sang or played the melody.
- The audience could do a little internal reflective work to deepen the emotional impact of some of the more serious Appalachian ballads.
- The audience could make up an additional verse to one of the sillier animal songs.

Seek to involve your audience in diverse and meaningful ways. If you find that your concert consists of one basic activity type, go back to Chapter 4 and find creative alternatives. Try to avoid using any of the activity archetypes more than once during a concert.

❧ PITFALL #8: The Presentation or the Interactions Are Unsuitable for the Specific Audience

Let's face it: retired Teamsters may not feel like standing up and touching their toes, and students older than eight may feel insulted if you ask them to sing "Twinkle, Twinkle, Little Star." Conversely, an unschooled listener may not find the unconventional modulations of Prokofiev's Classical Symphony as hilarious as a highly trained musician with perfect pitch does. Activities involving basic physical coordination skills may be too challenging for very young audiences but regarded as "babyish" by listeners who are only a few years older.

As musicians, it's hard to be experts on every audience demographic. Consequently, we sometimes give our listeners too little or too much credit. When in doubt whether an activity, topic, or explanation is appropriate, consult people from your audience's demographic. If you cannot consult prospective audience members directly, consult someone with a thorough understanding and knowledge of their tastes and abilities. Teachers, parents, children, and professors of cognitive development or educational psychology are all wonderful resources.

When in doubt whether an activity, topic, or explanation is appropriate, consult people from your audience's demographic.

Leonard Bernstein's Young People's Concerts provide fine examples of intelligent programming.
Photo credit: Eugene Cook; photo courtesy of the New York Philharmonic Archives

When you design an interactive performance, put yourself in your audience's shoes. Would you find the interactions fun and intriguing, or would you find them embarrassing, condescending, or overwhelmingly complex?

A jazz ensemble performing a lecture performance for a high school audience fell into this pitfall. The ensemble was knowledgeable and amazing, but their highly sophisticated and theoretical explanations went way over the audience's head until a young man raised his hand and said, "I don't get what you mean by that."

After a brief exchange, the leader of the band realized that the audience did not consist primarily of jazz students, as he had presumed. He proceeded to speak without jargon and accompanied his demonstrations with metaphors that made more sense to his listeners.

Through experience, you will develop an intuitive feel for what's right for any particular audience. In performance, be sensitive to your audience's reactions and make adjustments accordingly.

✗ PITFALL #9: The Musical Selections Are Too Long or Too Short

Plan your musical selections the same way you would plan any other concert or recital. Think about pacing, style, and the overall shape. If you were to remove all the interactions and have nothing but the music, would your chosen repertoire make a good CD or recital program?

Leonard Bernstein's televised Young People's Concerts arguably provide the finest examples of intelligent programming. Bernstein had an uncanny sense for ordering his selections and choosing works of an appropriate length. Consequently, each Young People's Concert feels like a satisfying musical experience as well as an enlightening educational event. Moreover, Bernstein also set the repertoire bar high by programming challenging contemporary works alongside timeless classics. Bernstein never "dumbed down."

So what is too long or too short?

It's difficult to establish hard-fast rules, but based on experience and Bernstein's example, in an orchestral situation, eight minutes seems to be a reasonable limit for what a young or inexperienced audience can comfortably digest. At the other end of the spectrum, too many selections under three minutes can feel like watching an endless stream of television commercials. Create a balance between longer works and shorter ones. When performing longer selections, it can help to let the audience know the approximate duration.

Sometimes in planning concerts, performers must confront the issue of making cuts. Some musicians maintain a deep philosophical aversion to making any cuts. That's fine; just be aware that longer durations place more demands on your audience's attention, so choose your repertoire accordingly. On occasion, I have lost the attention of some audience members by programming works that were too long for them. Once their focus had lapsed, it was very hard to regain it.

Bernstein did make cuts, and once again, he sets a superlative example. Most of the time, unless you have a score in front of you, you will not even realize that he has made a cut. If you do make cuts, strive to make them as unobtrusive as possible.

⚔ PITFALL #10: One or More Performers Are Disengaged

We've all seen it. A dynamic group leader is doing an outstanding job of communicating the joy of music and engaging her audience while the rest of the group is slouching, looking bored, or projecting an attitude of inattention and disinterest. More often than not, this disengaged appearance is the result of shyness, inexperience, or obliviousness rather than belligerence.

To rectify this situation, the leader should use her dynamic communication skills to draw out the more reticent performers. I'm a firm believer in actively involving every member of a small chamber ensemble at least once during a concert. Even if a performer is not comfortable speaking, he can participate when the audience is participating or help lead activities nonverbally. Often the very act of joining in for one activity will keep a performer more interested throughout the rest of the event.

In large ensemble or orchestral situations, look for ways to involve the entire ensemble in a large-group activity, and ask willing volunteers to come forward to lead various parts of the presentation.

If you still find yourself in a group of chronic slouchers, please stress to them—better yet, have an objective observer of your dress rehearsal stress to them—how important it is to look alert, smile, make eye contact with the audience, participate in activities, and remain visibly focused on whatever is happening at the moment. Better still, videotape a rehearsal and let people see their demeanors for themselves.

Don't settle for apathy. Inaction speaks louder than words.

Reaching Further: In-Depth Approaches

Arts organizations everywhere are working to increase the depth and scope of their outreach programs. Isolated "one-shot" events are gradually being replaced by residencies and programs that offer multiple artistic encounters, which are accompanied by preparation, creative participation, and follow-up. One of the primary reasons behind this dramatic shift is the realization that people cannot become lifelong participants and supporters of the arts through random, isolated experiences. However, if artistic encounters happen within the context of ongoing experience and immersion in the arts, they tend to have a substantial and meaningful impact.

As interactive performers, we should strive to maximize the impact of our work by deepening our approach. On the most basic level, we can extend the reach of our performances by preceding and following each concert with a related event or workshop.

> As interactive performers, we should strive to maximize the impact of our work by deepening our approach.

Preconcert Workshops

The Cooperstown Chamber Music Festival precedes its family concerts with a workshop based on the concert theme and follows the performance with an "instrument petting zoo" where the performers help audience members try out instruments.[1]

At one of the festival's family concerts featuring Copland's complete *Appalachian Spring* for thirteen instruments, the musicians offered a one-hour, multi-station preparatory workshop. The walls were covered with mural paper and the audience was invited to add their own drawings to create a panoramic picture of the rural American landscape. Folk dancers taught people dance steps for the Shaker melody "Simple Gifts," as a violinist from the ensemble performed it. At another station, the concertgoers made "musical quilts" by gluing leather musical notes, fabric, and symbols to muslin sheets. Once a quilt was finished, it could be taken to a musician who would perform the notes. After the concert, children took their quilt squares home as a souvenir.

The musicians also held a "musical Olympics" where they competed to see who could play the loudest, the fastest, the softest, and so forth. All the events

---

[1] Linda Chesis, artistic director and flutist, states that students have returned in subsequent years to report that they now take lessons playing an instrument they had tried out the year before.

Preconcert activities at the Cooperstown Chamber Music Festival. Photo courtesy of Linda Chesis

of the preconcert workshop served either to highlight the contextual mood of Copland's work or to introduce the instruments and the themes they would play. Consequently, the audience was able to focus for the entire uninterrupted performance of the work.

The preconcert workshop approach works for adults as well. In a program titled *Samba vs. Tango: The Cultural Contrasts of South America*,[2] Chris Perry and Erin Furbee of the Oregon Symphony put together an incredible six-station preconcert workshop. Ticket-buyers could learn to tango, go to samba school, try out Latin percussion instruments, watch a slideshow of Carnival images, try on Carnival costumes, and meet a strolling bandoneon player who demonstrated his instrument and answered questions. To ensure attendance of the preconcert event, tickets announced the starting time as 7:00 pm (the time of the workshop), although the performance itself began at 8:00. Given the fun nature of the activities—and the free, thematic food and drinks—patrons responded with delight at the unanticipated surprise.

As enjoyable as the preconcert activities were, they were not just games and light entertainment. Most of them cleverly familiarized listeners with the rhythms, timbres, instruments, and genres they would hear during the concert. The workshop was a preparation as much as it was a party.

---

[2] For a complete description of this program, see Eric Booth's article "Edifications: Fuller Audience Engagement: Sure, But What Does It Look Like?" *Chamber Music* 20, no. 3 (June 2003): 22–23. *Chamber Music*'s *Edifications* column is a great resource for interactive concert ideas.

CONSIDER THIS

With a little planning, you can create fun events and workshops to precede or follow your concerts. Here is a brief list of offerings that have proven enjoyable for a wide range of audiences.

- Stations for trying real instruments or building homemade ones.
- Mini-performances by musicians, actors, dancers, or storytellers.
- Opportunities to interact with musicians and composers.
- Music or dance lessons.

- Workshops that prepare the audience for an opportunity to perform in the concert.
- Workshops where people compose something to be performed during the concert.
- Food and drink.
- Mementos or "gift bags" that can be taken home. Be sure to include a bumper sticker or other appropriate items promoting your ensemble.

Concert Series

As phenomenal as a single event may be, for long-term impact, the audience needs repeated musical experiences. Try creating a series of at least three interactive concerts. For maximum effect, have each build or expand on the material of the preceding concert. Create annually recurring events and find ways to promote them.

Also start thinking about ways of reaching your audiences before the day of the event. When partnering with schools and other organizations, you can deepen the concert experience by offering preparatory workshops and literature in the days preceding the performance.

At the Hudson Valley Philharmonic, classroom teachers receive a study guide of preparatory activities, as well as recorded excerpts of the concert repertoire. (Helpful hint: The guides and recordings are most likely to be used if they are sent to the music teachers.) To help teachers use the study guide most effectively, Teaching Artists offer teachers' workshops where they lead teachers through the activities step by step.

After the classroom teacher has prepared the students, a Teaching Artist or an ensemble visits the school and leads a workshop and performance for students. Having been thoroughly prepared, students attend the fully interactive orchestra concert. Following the event, teachers and Teaching Artists can help students reflect on the event by leading follow-up activities from the teachers' guide.

Short-Term Residency

For an even deeper approach, you can develop a short-term, intensive residency at one location. Andrew Appel of the Baroque chamber group The Four Nations Ensemble has developed a highly successful weeklong model for working in public schools.

The Four Nations Ensemble in residence in the South Bronx. Photo credit: David Rodgers

Every morning, The Four Nations Ensemble performs a concert for the entire school. During the day, the ensemble members visit individual classrooms where they lead hands-on workshops. The students practice listening skills, discuss what they hear, share their interpretations with one another, and draw pictures inspired by music.

One ingenious aspect of The Four Nations Ensemble's approach is its strategy for developing attention spans. The first assembly performance is brief and introductory. With each following day, the duration of the morning performance is incrementally increased. By the end of the week, the students are ready to focus for a full forty-five-minute musical performance.

On the last day, students, teachers, and principals express how much they wish the ensemble could become a permanent part of the school. The residency culminates in a Saturday concert with the local orchestra, which buses the students and their parents to the concert hall.

Long-Term Partnerships and Residencies

The most intensive outreach programs entail long-term partnerships and residencies. While we often look to larger arts organizations to provide communities with such programs, individual musicians and groups are capable of designing long-term residencies as well. The Ying Quartet has achieved wide acclaim for its incredibly in-depth, multiyear community residencies sponsored by the National Endowment for the Arts, Chamber Music America, and other organizations.

When the Yings are in residence, they work hard to reach every part of the community. In addition to their evening concert series, the group gives workshops and performances in every conceivable venue: churches, hospitals, schools, businesses, homes, social clubs, and more. By the end of the residency, the entire community embraces the quartet and its music. The experience is rewarding for the quartet as well, and it makes a point of returning to perform in the years following the residency.

If you want to have the same kind of impact in your community, begin strategizing a community outreach plan today. Define your purpose as a musician, ensemble, or organization, and determine whom you most desire to target in your community. It is better to do a thorough, in-depth job of reaching a smaller segment of the population than to try to reach all of the people in a limited, scattershot fashion.

Once you have a plan, seek sponsors and apply for grants with local, state, and national arts councils. There is a significant amount of available aid, but it must be pursued. If you can hire a professional grant writer or development director, you will likely save yourself time while receiving more funding than you might discover on your own. Many grant writers will work on a per hour or per project basis.

In addition to assistance with the financial part of outreach, professional development for concert design and presentation is gradually becoming available. As musicians become more and more skilled in this work, growing numbers of mentors and consultants are available to help others. Chamber Music America, the American Symphony Orchestra League, and various Arts in Education organizations provide workshops, seminars, and forums for improving our presentational, planning, and marketing skills.

In-depth approaches clearly require considerable planning and vision, but the dividends are well worth the investment. In time, we can build enduring relationships in our community and foster a lifelong love of music in our audiences. And if we accomplish that, our art will always have a future.

Reaching Out in the Real World

When I give interactive concert workshops and performances, most musicians express an appreciation for the ideas and strategies shared in this book. However, the thought of taking the information and applying it themselves often raises questions and concerns. Because you probably are wondering some of the same things, let's address the most common concerns.

If you've never done anything like this before, how do you get started?

If you are excited about the possibilities and confident in your presentational abilities, go ahead and plan a wholeheartedly interactive event. If you feel a little cautious or unsure about interacting, start gradually. If possible, perform with musicians who are successful with this approach. Let them take the lead, but ask to have an active role during the performance.

If you are working on your own, try giving a recital where you speak a few sentences before each piece. When that feels comfortable, include one to two simple audience-participation activities. As time goes on, you will become bolder and more comfortable with what you're doing.

How do you get good at this? I know some people who are naturals, but not everybody's good at this . . .

Interactive performance is a discipline and an art in its own right. As with musical performance, the skills and techniques must be learned, developed, and practiced. The more you practice, the better you become and the easier it gets.

> Interactive performance is a discipline and an art in its own right

You can also become better by studying the work of others. When I first began having residencies as a Teaching Artist, I relied heavily on the example of experienced colleagues. I read their lesson plans; I incorporated their best activities into my workshops; I asked them questions whenever I ran into problems. In short, I modeled my work after the best practices I knew.

When I was hired to stand in front of a full orchestra and lead an interactive concert, I saw as many educational concerts as I possibly could. I viewed videotapes of Leonard Bernstein's Young People's Concerts, Wynton Marsalis's *Marsalis on Music*, and other music education programs. I attended events in public schools; I went to children's concerts by various organizations. I took notes on what worked and what bombed. I tried to ascertain why. I interviewed people who attended the events and studied their reactions. Whenever possible, I spoke to the producers of the event to find out their intentions and their assessment of the actual concert.

Wynton Marsalis reaches out during Jazz @ Lincoln Center's *Jazz for Young People* concerts. Photo credit: Frank Stewart

Become a good interactive performer by learning from people who excel at it. Note what not to do whenever something doesn't go so well. Granted, some people are more predisposed to this way of working than others. Fortunately, with a little effort, we all can improve our abilities, regardless of what our overall level is at the moment.

Application

One of the safest ways to interact is to take a successful activity that you have observed and lead it yourself. Go back to Chapter 4 or read the scripts in Appendix A to find ideas that you would feel comfortable trying. Try them out in a safe environment where failure isn't critical. Ask your family to be a "guinea pig" audience. Volunteer to perform at a senior center or your former elementary school. Practice.

Perhaps the key to improvement is maintaining a commitment to lifelong learning. We must choose to keep getting better at engaging audiences throughout our careers, never settling for the ways we currently do things, and never assuming that what we do now is good enough. The field requires that we keep pressing forward so that we can share our art most effectively. We should model a life of ongoing inquiry and musical curiosity for our fellow musicians so that they, too, can improve.

If your concerns are mostly about speaking in front of a group, try taking a public speaking course or an acting course at your local community college. You can also join Toastmasters or other organizations devoted to honing speaking skills. Explore ways to interact with as few words as possible—many activities can be done without any words at all.

I believe in the interactive approach, but my group doesn't get it. They're impossible. How do I deal with them?

If I had a nickel for every time someone has raised this issue, I could buy us both a new glockenspiel.

There is no single solution to this problem; your plan of action must be tailored to the personalities and problems of your individual group. I will share a few success stories from colleagues in the field.[3] Perhaps the troublesome aspects of their situations will apply to yours.

Rebecca was a member of a fairly large group of chamber players who gave frequent performances in public schools, particularly middle schools. The senior members of the group favored a traditional lecture approach, which never seemed to connect with the students. On the way home, the ensemble would complain about how rotten today's youth are.

When Rebecca couldn't stand this pattern any longer, she told the group, "Look, let me lead the next concert, and let me do it my way. If it's a disaster, I'll take full responsibility, but give me the chance to experiment because the way we're doing things right now isn't working."

Rebecca was given carte blanche to design and host the next event. Because her approach proved a vast improvement over the status quo, the group gladly delegated responsibility for planning and scripting the concerts to her.

Rebecca felt she needed to use this confrontational approach because previously, she was not in a position of control or influence. If you find that you have no bearing on your group's concerts, you may need to assert yourself and offer to lead for a change.

Allison, a quartet violist, had quite a different problem. She was the driving creative force behind her ensemble's interactive concert, and her first violinist was enthusiastic and supportive of everything she wanted to do. However, the second violinist and the cellist were, in her words, "Dead. They just sit there and act like they don't care about anything. I want to strangle them!"

The musicians in question were incredible players, but they had rarely given any performances outside of traditional recitals and concerts. Allison was taking them into totally unfamiliar territory, and they were understandably uncomfortable and reluctant to participate.

Allison solved her problems by enlisting help from outside the group. She asked two qualified musician coaches to attend the dress rehearsal and provide feedback. The observers offered praise and constructive suggestions to all of the musicians. Nonthreatening participatory roles were created for the reluctant partners. After the concert, the previously unforthcoming musicians came to appreciate Allison's approach, and they seemed open to trying similar events in the future.

If you struggle with disengagement within your group, sometimes an outside voice will prove effective in motivating unresponsive members.

---

[3] To protect the anonymity of the individuals, ensembles, and organizations, all the names have been changed.

Manny was frustrated by a group member who participated in counterproductive ways. "Every time we play a community concert, Edgar goes off on these long, boring biographies about the composer, or he gives these non sequitur monologues on stuff like 'why classical music is important.' It's so embarrassing, it makes the rest of us cringe!"

Manny's case is particularly complicated because his ensemble has a resident boor. Boors seldom realize that they are being boorish. There is no tactful way to alert them, nor is there any guarantee that they will believe you or behave any differently if you do.

One of the best ways to reign in boors and other verbal transgressors is to formally script your event, and hold all members to the script. If anyone balks, explain that your presentation has extremely limited time, and you want to make sure everything gets covered.

If your "Edgar" needs to have input into the script in order to feel personally validated, so be it. If his proposed text strays from your theme into less relevant areas, simply say something like, "That's great, Edgar, but we're getting away from the music here. . . . I want to be sure that everything we do helps our audience to *hear* what comes next." If he digresses during the concert, try tactfully interrupting him with an interjection that keeps the group on-course.

Videotape your concert. Watch and discuss it as a group. When people watch themselves, they often can see their own shortcomings more clearly than they can onstage. If possible, watch the video with someone outside the group who hasn't seen the program before. Again, outsiders can provide input in ways that group members can't without jeopardizing group chemistry or relationships.

Stacy, an education director of a "big five" orchestra, found himself in a position where some members of his orchestra were philosophically opposed to any kind of interaction. As they saw it, audience-centered approaches turned the focus away from the orchestra and departed too much from the regular concertgoing experience.

Stacy listened to their concerns and undertook several initiatives to address them. To acknowledge the dissenting musicians' preference for more traditional ways of connecting with the public, he provided opportunities for them to give master classes, preconcert lectures, and postconcert talks. By doing so, he helped them to participate in outreach efforts that corresponded with their own views. Rather than ignore noncompliant individuals, Stacy made sure that every musician had a way to contribute successfully to the orchestra's education mission.

To test the validity of his interactive approaches, as well as the musicians' concerns, he hired an independent firm to formally poll audience members who had attended the interactive events. Over 75 percent of the audience members polled were enthusiastic about the new, interactive approach. Of the remaining 25 percent, roughly 3 percent responded negatively. Stacy presented the report to the orchestra committee, who consented that the new approach must be working.

I should mention that from the beginning, Stacy enlisted like-minded orchestra members to participate in his events and bolster support for his efforts. To effect philosophical change within an organization, you must have advocates and allies, as well as an ongoing, intraensemble communication plan for sharing the experiments and their impact. Little by little, institutional change can occur.

Jessica encountered Stacy's problem, but within a woodwind quintet. Two members violently opposed any audience participation; they preferred a presentational information-based approach, which Jessica often found condescending in tone. For various reasons, she did not feel that she had the liberty to use the bold, take-control approach Rebecca had employed with her group.

Jessica ultimately used a gradual, oblique strategy for steering her ensemble to a more audience-centered approach. She decided to perform a series of interactive recitals with her oboe and piano duo. She invited her quintet to attend, and little by little, they came to understand her ideas and perspective.

Currently, the quintet still gives fairly conventional community performances, but for each one, the quintet allows Jessica to lead one or two participatory activities. Although the performances are still not as interactive as Jessica would like, they are more so than they were two years earlier.

What do you do if you find yourself in a really tough situation, like a school where the kids misbehave?

Sometimes it's fun to sit around with musicians sharing our "nightmares from the field" in a game of "Can you top this?" Every challenging situation demands a unique response, but usually there is a way to overcome (or at the minimum, survive) even the most challenging situations.

The first thing any group or organization should do is to take proactive measures to prevent a potentially bad situation. Put a reasonable cap on audience size. For children's concerts, require an appropriate number of adult chaperones. Have a nursery or a "crying room" for infants. Send participating organizations a preparatory packet that includes friendly information about the concert etiquette you expect. During the concert, abide by subtle control measures like saying, "I'm only going to pick volunteers who are sitting still and not calling out! . . . oh, I love the way you're sitting quietly—you'll be our first volunteer!"

Also, check the attitudes of your colleagues, your ushers, and security guards. Do your voices and body language project warmth and enthusiasm, or do they exude fear, discomfort, disdain, or a wish that you were elsewhere? If anyone projects the latter attitudes, don't expect your audience to enjoy being with you.

CONSIDER THIS

Do your words treat the audience with respect, or are you unconsciously condescending or perpetuating unhealthy preconceptions and stereotypes? I once saw a performer tell an inner-city eighth-grade audience, "The bell's going to ring during this last number, but we'll keep playing. If you go out softly, you'll hear the end of it. Sneak out like you've just robbed a house!"

A few students gasped incredulously, and others snickered and murmured. While the performer was probably trying to be "cool" or funny, his unfortunate remark insulted his audience by reinforcing implicit socioeconomic and racial prejudices.

Within your concert interactions, include control measures. Teach a quiet signal or use a conductor's cutoff signal. Be sure that the audience has settled down before you perform anything.

Even if your ensemble has an ideal attitude and preventative measures have been taken, behavior problems can still surface. Sometimes, the best response is to ignore the situation and let the appropriate authorities reprimand the offenders.

If no authority is present or competent, however, you may have to solve the problem yourself. During one performance, I encountered a fourth grader in the front row who scowled, grimaced, and sat with his hands over his ears for the duration of the first piece. It became clear that this boy was determined to give a defiant performance of his own.

My next piece required a volunteer to play the drums. Instinctively, I selected the scowler when he volunteered. Instead of clowning, he took his role seriously, returned to his seat, and behaved for the rest of the concert. His misbehavior had apparently stemmed from an unspoken need for attention, and once I addressed it, he could function properly.

On occasion, an entire audience can get out of hand. Although I like to get audiences excited about music, I must be careful not to overexcite them. After one particularly fun activity, a third-grade audience became a little too talkative and rowdy. The guitarist in my group restored order by raising his hand and firmly saying, "We can't go on until everyone calms down." We waited patiently until the students regained their composure, then proceeded without problem.

How do you do interactive concerts for adults?

All of the strategies and ideas presented in this book can prove effective with virtually any audience. However, the way you present the material may need to be adjusted according to the age and the venue. Naturally, adults should be treated as adults. You should also assume that some of them may have no formal musical knowledge, whereas others may have extensive musical backgrounds.

In some venues, such as comedy clubs, the environment is so open and participatory that it would almost be strange or rude not to interact or experiment. Comedy showcases are particularly good places to try out five- to ten-minute self-contained performances in-between acts. The instant feedback is incredible.

In a more staid environment (e.g., a recital hall) or a more social environment (e.g., a noisy club), you may need to adjust your approach. Unless adults bring children, they initially may be less prone to indulge in creative participatory activities, but if you establish your out-of-the-ordinary expectations from the beginning and win the audience over with a "low-threat" activity that has a significant payoff, you'll discover how readily people will adapt to your approach. Some types of activities will be more comfortable and conducive to particular venues than others.

CONSIDER THIS

Often adults prove shyer than children when it comes to answering or asking questions in front of others. Following a dress rehearsal of an interactive performance designed for adults, a colleague commented on a particular phenomenon he has noticed. When he leads workshops and interactive performances for adults, his initial question is usually met by an awkward silence. Once that first question is answered, people participate more willingly.

As several of us confirmed that we shared the same experience, we wondered why this hesitation happens and what we could do about it. We concluded that this phenomenon stems from a couple of fairly obvious factors:

1. Nobody wants to appear foolish by giving a wrong or weird answer in front of a group of peers.
2. Having an expert ask for input from his audience is quite a departure from the traditional arts appreciation/lecture model. Consequently, it takes people a moment to adjust their expectations.

Out of our discussion some useful strategies for shortening the silence and increasing comfort with interaction emerged:

- Make your first question a "softball" (an easy question—probably one without wrong answers or one that requires no extensive expertise).
- Ask the first question in a way that it can be answered communally (e.g., by a show of hands or a unison verbal response).
- Poll the audience on their familiarity with the subject and set up a context for sharing. ("Raise your hands if this is your first encounter with the music of Elliott Carter. . . . Okay, now raise your hands if you've heard a work or two of his or know a bit about him. . . . Now, raise your hands if you're a diehard Elliott Carter fan. Good. Over the next half-hour, we'll be drawing on each others' perceptions and expertise so that we all can hear what's great about this composer.)
- Frame the event differently to set up your expectations. To switch from a standard preconcert lecture to something more interactive, the Los Angeles Philharmonic set up microphones in the audience to suggest more of a talk-show environment. To take some of the formality and pressure off the host as well as the audience, the event was titled "Casual Talk," and the location was an open space where people could feel free to join the activities late.
- If adults are hesitating when you ask for something like conducting, humming, or clapping, assure them that actively participating will make a big difference in their ability to hear and feel the music.
- Model the participation in a way that encourages people to join in.

In general, adults have a deeper hunger for information—particularly information on how the music works—and they expect interaction to be focused in a specific direction. Composer, pianist, and commentator Robert Kapilow has built quite a following with a lecture series called *What Makes It Great?* in which he and his performers thoroughly investigate a musical masterwork the day before a concert. Kapilow's audience is almost entirely adult, yet anyone attending can count on singing, taking part in musical experiments, or concentrating their utmost to meet the listening challenges that Kapilow gives. People keep returning and subscribing because Kapilow's participatory approach always helps listeners to discover details they would otherwise miss.

Application

Take an activity from a concert you have done for children, or choose an activity from a children's concert in Appendix A. How would you need to adjust the dialogue and the participation for an adult audience? for high school or middle school students?

I'd like to do this, but I'm overworked and can't find the time that it would take to revamp the programs I've been doing.

All of us are overworked, and none of us can find enough planning or practice time. Nevertheless, if we believe in the importance and relevance of audience interaction, we can make the time. If changing your approach is important to you, schedule time to work on it. Put pressure on yourself to follow through by booking and advertising an interactive performance. When a performance is pending, you can't avoid preparing.

To reiterate an earlier caution, when learning how to interact, don't undermine yourself and your self-confidence by underpreparing the interactive parts of your performance. Interacting is challenging enough because it is unconventional; don't make it harder by winging it. Plan and rehearse. You will increase your success and confidence by starting simply, but with thorough preparation.

If your time constraints result from obligations to your employers, be honest with them. If they are asking you to do community outreach concerts, but not providing adequate time or compensation, make your needs known in a cooperative way that demonstrates your willingness and your commitment to outreach efforts. Stress how important it is to make the best impression on your audience. Some musicians have been granted brief sabbaticals for honing their presentational skills and designing concerts. Work with your employers to reach acceptable solutions.

How do you recommend bringing orchestral musicians on-board when you're an education director or conductor who wants to involve them in interactive concerts?

Usually every orchestra has a core group of musicians who are eager to participate in educational initiatives or who are enthusiastic about communicating musical ideas. Identify these musicians and bring them into your team; some may prove to be excellent concert hosts, script writers, or even concert producers.

Of course, this kind of involvement requires an extra measure of dedication, and it takes time to develop relationships with these musicians. Moreover, even the most enthusiastic musicians may require training or supervision when beginning work in educational or interactive concerts.

If the musicians are not primarily responsible for scripting and hosting the concert, but they have active roles to play, it is best to prepare a one-page outline that lets them know exactly what to play at what time. The outline should clarify exactly what their participatory role is and when it happens. Go over the sheet in rehearsal, answer any questions, and be sure that each stand has a cue sheet for the concert. Outside the rehearsal or during a break, speak individually to any musicians with significant roles. Orchestral musicians greatly appreciate efficient preparation and certainty about what is expected of them.

Do we have to do something interactive for every piece of music?

Sometimes after seeing a demonstration of a fairly involved activity, a musician nervously asks, "That was really sophisticated. Do we have to do something like that before every piece?"

Let's get something straight: interaction is a choice, not a compulsion. As concert designer, you can decide how much or how little to interact. You interact not because you "should" or "must," but because effective interaction vitalizes the experience of the audience.

> Interaction is a choice, not a compulsion. You interact not because you "should" or "must," but because effective interaction vitalizes the experience of the audience.

Some pieces benefit from a fairly involved setup. Other works, particularly short selections, are best served by a quick and simple introduction. Remember that it is also possible to lead one powerful activity that focuses the listening for the next few selections, or even an entire concert.

At least once during a performance, I like to let the audience hear something without any preparatory activity at all. The key is to find a balance within your concert. Arrange your repertoire and interactions in such a way that the activity order is as pleasing as the musical order.

If you're a soloist or a chamber group who interacts, how do you get presenters to understand?

On the whole, presenters, especially for smaller, independent, and more regional venues, love to book performers who know how to engage their audiences. Some students tell me that many presenters now require them to talk to audiences in addition to performing an evening of music.

Performers and ensembles who know how to interact bring an extra dimension to a performance. Use your skills as an asset. Mention them in your press kit and publicity materials. Make your manager or agent aware of what you can do.

Interaction is best understood through experience, not description. If you can give a ten-minute demonstration that includes a brief preparatory activity and a performance, presenters will know exactly what you are offering, and they will buy it. Put together a five- to ten-minute video compilation of your best audience interactions, and film a few complete interactive concerts for sharing.

When you choose to make presenters aware of your intentions may depend on the situation. Often, interaction is a selling point, but if you sense you are dealing with conventional or conservative bookers, you may initially choose to hint at what you do, and reveal the full concept gradually. Appealing to familiar artists and approaches, like Leonard Bernstein's Young People's Concerts, or Yo-Yo Ma's *Inspired by Bach,* can help hesitant presenters to feel secure.

These techniques are great; can you tell me how to use them in other areas, like conducting my youth orchestra and teaching private lessons?

Most of the techniques presented in this book can be easily transferred to teaching situations, because this educational approach really originated in the classroom. When we apply these strategies to instrumental teaching, we and our students can benefit from an enriched appreciation for the music we are studying.

I think one of the major reasons for student attrition in private lessons and large ensembles is that students grow bored with rehearsing the same pieces over and over. When the focus becomes so centered on perfect execution, it's easy to forget what's great about the music.

To maintain student interest and learning via your new teaching perspectives, simply follow the activity-design procedure. Study the piece, find an entry point, and design activities appropriate for your learners.

When helping private students, look for ways to help them explore a concept or solve a musical problem in a creative way. Whenever possible, try to address multiple intelligences and different learning styles.

CONSIDER THIS

In private lessons, students sometimes benefit from an approach that departs from traditional pedagogy and addresses an intelligence other than musical intelligence. When I was in graduate school, I had the privilege of assisting Karen Tuttle with a very gifted studio of violists. Grace, a masters student, approached me for help with Zoltan Kodaly's transcription of J. S. Bach's *Chromatic Fantasy*, one of the most technically challenging pieces in the viola repertoire.

Grace had mastered all of the technical challenges of the piece, but she felt her performance was not as musically interesting as she would like. Rather than go through the piece and dictate my own interpretation, I asked her to choose a section that she particularly wanted to improve.

After she selected a passage of ascending and descending arpeggios, I handed her a blank sheet of paper and asked her to sketch the melodic contour with a magic marker. When her graphic notation was finished, I asked her to improvise music that followed the shape of the contours. The only rule I imposed was that she couldn't use any of Bach's notes.

When she was comfortable interpreting the contours by improvising scales and arpeggios, I asked her to take the next step of writing various moods, dynamics, and emotions for each line. After improvising and experimenting with the various options, she returned to Bach's original and played her chosen passage with spirit and emotional flair. Our experiments away from the piece had sharpened her sense of the musical possibilities within Bach's sweeping arpeggios.

Students in orchestras, bands, and choirs enjoy using their instruments and voices in creative, exploratory ways. Some directors nurture students' musical interest by taking one or two Fridays a month to lead a workshop related to one of the pieces that's being performed. For examples of the kinds of workshops you could lead, see the New York Philharmonic's *Special Editions for Teachers*.[4]

Does every performance have to be interactive?

As Solomon said, "To everything there is a season and a time for every purpose under heaven." In every situation, you will need to decide for yourself how much or how little to interact, as well as how to do so.

Every performance is a transaction between performer and listener. Some performances, like major recital debuts, have traditionally maintained a very formal delineation between the two. Personally, I hope that someday a bold performer will surprise audiences and critics alike with a debut that showcases powerful communication skills as well as musical and instrumental prowess.

Interaction increases your odds of connecting with your listeners. By breaking down the imaginary wall between you and your audience, listeners get to know and appreciate who you are as a human being. With few exceptions, people enjoy this relationship, and they are more likely to return to hear you again. Effective interaction is rewarding for everyone involved.

> Interaction increases your odds of connecting with your listeners.

Let's not forget that the primary reason for interacting is to enhance the audience's perceptions of the music. You are in a unique position to help the audience discover greatness in your repertoire. Your extra efforts will help listeners to hear more than they would otherwise. Not all music reveals itself on the first hearing, and sometimes, no amount of talking about it will do any good. Successful hearing will depend on your giving the audience a perceptual experience.

While the purposes of some performances suggest more interactivity than others, every performance should seek to engage the audience. Interactive approaches simply give you more exciting options for accomplishing this objective.

One balanced approach that works well with long-term residencies is to give a series of interactive concerts or workshops at various locations as a preview, preparation, and advertisement for a formal evening concert. Through this approach, people become familiar with the group and learn how to hear its music before attending a more standard concert event. The audience has been engaged in advance, and listeners can connect to the music in ways that would not be possible without preparation.

Assess each situation individually. With experience, you'll know what's right.

---

[4] See Appendix C for citations for *An American Celebration, Bernstein Live*, and *Pathways to the Orchestra.*

Reaching Out Every Day

Occasionally, musicians wax nostalgic about a time when there were music teachers, instrumental programs, and performing ensembles in practically every school. Sometimes, the wistfulness gives way to resentment about the extra demands made on professionally performing musicians as arts organizations try to fill the educational voids. Some musicians maintain that if music education (or the administrators who handle fund-raising, public relations, advertising, and audience development) were everything it should be, professional musicians could be relieved of their outreach responsibilities. This view raises an important question:

If we had better, more universal music education in this country, would interactive performances still be necessary?

Absolutely. Even if effective music education programs are in place (may they ever be!), artists cannot afford to shirk their responsibility to reach out to audiences. Remember, during the golden age of music education in America, Leonard Bernstein still sensed a profound need to educate and cultivate audiences. Judging from the vivid reminiscences of those who grew up on Bernstein's concerts, his efforts were well spent.

In the best of circumstances, artists still must learn to interact with the public if they are to have a constituency and be part of the community. Pamela Link, an outstanding public school music teacher from Boise, Idaho, recently took a one-year sabbatical to visit New York City and study various Teaching Artist-centered outreach programs. Why? Even with flagship music education programs in the Boise public schools, many graduates of the system were not continuing musical involvement on graduation, and the city's professional orchestra grappled with the same audience-development issues as cities where music education was virtually nonexistent. Pam hopes that the development of artist-led outreach programs that involve symphony musicians will bridge the gap between successful traditional music education and lifelong musical participation.

Recent research from the Lila Wallace Foundation concludes that the future of the arts depends on changing our sense of what participation in the arts means.[5] The foundation recommends that artists

1. deepen the experience of the existing arts-goers;
2. broaden their contact with people who are like current arts-goers; and
3. diversify to include new kinds of people in their audiences.

---

[5] Walker, Chris, and Stephanie Scott-Melnyk, with Kay Sherwood. *Reggae to Rachmaninoff: How and Why People Participate in Arts and Culture.* Washington D.C.: The Urban Institute, 2002.

Interactive performance is one of the rare ideas that can accomplish all three objectives at the same occasion. Interaction can deepen the level of engagement of sophisticated audiences, broaden the appeal to make newcomers feel successful, and engage diverse audiences through the universal effectiveness of hands-on understanding.

Interaction can deepen the level of engagement of sophisticated audiences, broaden the appeal to make newcomers feel successful, and engage diverse audiences through the universal effectiveness of hands-on understanding.

Clearly, we cannot depend on others to build relationships between us and our audiences. To build these relationships, *we* must interact; we must reach out.

Ideally, reaching out is more than a performance strategy; it's an approach to life. The more adept we become at sharing our music with others, the more we will realize that we have daily opportunities to be advocates and ambassadors for our art. Some of the most inspired musicians I know seek to have musical conversations with total strangers. Others get out their instruments to demonstrate them for inquisitive children who are riding on the same train car. To these musicians, everybody is a potential listener, music-lover, subscriber, board member, private student, or colleague.

David Cerone, violinist and president of the Cleveland Institute of Music, likes to tell his students, "You are in the communication business." The thought initially disconcerts some students—didn't they go to a conservatory to perfect their technique and musicianship so that they could win auditions and competitions? Isn't being a musician about making music? Sooner or later, however, the students realize that musicians must devote considerable attention to the audience side of the equation if their art form is to survive.

We are in the communication business. With our instruments and voices, we convey the innermost thoughts and emotions of some of the greatest minds the world will ever know. Unless we learn to present great works with the same artistry, integrity, and creativity with which we perform them, the masterpieces we play will not be heard, appreciated, or understood by everyone in our audiences.

To fully communicate, we must engage our audiences in ways that heighten their perceptions and emotions. We must formulate long-term plans for cultivating musical understanding and for developing and maintaining relationships with the audiences in our communities. Nobody else is going to do it for us.

If we rise to the challenge creatively, however, our responsibility becomes a joy, not a burden. As we seek to convey the greatness of a musical work, we immerse ourselves in the work and rediscover its greatness for ourselves. How wonderful it is to return to pieces we have performed for years and formulate new insights or notice details we had previously overlooked. How incredible it is when we enable an audience to listen with the same sense of awe and discovery!

As we learn to interact in meaningful ways, our musical understanding grows with our audience's. We help our listeners to hear our insights. They help us to hear theirs. We revisit our pieces with new perspectives and intriguing questions, and the cycle continues.

Our capacity to share music with our audiences is in direct proportion to our own musical curiosity and passion. If we cultivate these two faculties, we shall always have something to communicate, we shall always maintain our musical enthusiasm, and we shall always have a fervor for helping others to hear. Our audiences will truly listen, and we will never settle for anything less.

Appendix A
Five Interactive Concert Transcripts

No book on interactive performance would be complete without real-life transcripts of concerts that worked. Following are five transcripts that illustrate the primary types of interactive concerts you are likely to design: concerts about composers, inquiry-driven concerts focused on developing listening skills and musical understanding, and thematic concerts with natural curricular ties to learning and literacy standards. Regardless of its overall theme, each concert seeks to illuminate specific repertoire through strategic activities.

These transcripts represent performances for a variety of audiences at considerably different venues. The activities and dialogue vary accordingly; hopefully, you will get a clear sense of what interaction looks like under different circumstances. The introduction to each concert explains its particular context.

All of the scripts are protected by copyright law, but if you are interested in performing all or part of a particular concert, a license can be arranged.

Application

After you have read through the transcripts, reexamine them. What entry point is chosen for any given piece? What activity gave the audience an experience of it? What are some other possible entry points and activities? What interactive archetypes are used? Are there new strategies that weren't mentioned previously? The more you analyze the choices an interactive performer makes, the better you'll become at understanding and applying your own interactive skills.

What's So Great About Mozart?

Building a concert around a composer is one of the most common strategies for creating an interactive or educational concert. In composer-based concerts, presenters often focus on sharing biographical and contextual information about the composer and his or her works. While such information can be helpful, the most artistically successful composer-centered concerts involve some kind of intriguing inquiry: How does Copland create an American sound? What made Stravinsky radical? Or in this case, What's so great about Mozart? The right inquiry enables the audience to understand the composer's style and sound—not just the biographical context.

What's So Great About Mozart? was a Kids' Concert performed by the musicians of the Bridgehampton Chamber Music Festival. Children at these concerts are typically preschool age, or slightly older, but artistic director Marya Martin rightly insists that these family concerts be engaging for older siblings, adults, and the festival musicians as well. I like to think of the old Warner Brothers cartoons, which appealed to children, but which also had subtle inside jokes and cultural references for parents' amusement.

The Bridgehampton concerts take place in a wooden Presbyterian church that seats approximately 250 people. The intimate nature of the venue allows for considerable interaction, hands-on inquiry, discussion, and even small-group work. All of the musical cues for this concert were worked out in advance, but the BCMF musicians' responses were spontaneous and unscripted.

Many thanks to composer Eric Ewazen for the "rapid-fire solfeggio lesson" activity!

What's So Great About Mozart? A Concert for the Bridgehampton Chamber Music Festival

Marya Martin, flute
Soovin Kim, violin
Roberto Diaz, viola
Andres Diaz, cello
Philip Bush, piano
David Wallace, host

Program:

> W. A. Mozart: Piano Quartet in E-flat Major, K. 493:

I. Allegro
III. Allegretto

> Flute Quartet in D Major, K. 285, III. Rhondo
> "Ein Mädchen oder Weibchen" from *The Magic Flute*
> Paul Reale: Piano Trio (1980), III. Mozart

Materials:

> Assorted percussion
> Metallophone tuned to a C major scale
> Giant "Ein Mädchen oder Weibchen" vocal melody score
> "Ein Mädchen oder Weibchen" melody and piano vocal score for musicians
> Recitative music for musicians
> "Ein Mädchen oder Weibchen" in major and minor for musicians
> Microphone to be used as a prop

MUSICIANS ENTER, BOW, AND PERFORM THE EXPOSITION OF THE FIRST MOVEMENT OF K. 493.

David: Good evening, and welcome, everybody! We just heard some music by a man named Mozart—Wolfgang Amadeus Mozart. Raise your hand if you've ever heard of him or listened to his music. Today's concert is called *What's So Great About Mozart?* and we're going to share some of the secrets of his greatness, but first I'd like to ask you all, what's so great about Mozart? Who was he, and what do you know about him?

Child #1: He was a famous composer.

David: Good! A famous person who wrote music. What else?

Child #2: He wrote his first piece when he was four years old.

Child #3: Um . . . he's my *favorite* composer!

David (raising hand): How many of the rest of you would say he's your favorite composer? Well alright! One of the things that helped Mozart to be a great composer is that he was a terrific pianist. How many of you are five years old or younger? By the time Mozart was five years old, he was such a great pianist that kings and queens were inviting him to their palaces to play for them. They gave him chocolate and presents, so he thought that was pretty neat. When he was older, people said he was one of the best pianists in the whole world, and also one of the best violinists and violists. Who can tell me how you become one of the best musicians in the world?

Child #4: You practice!

David: You practice! That's right, and one of the most important things to practice is what we call scales—patterns that go up and down and sound like this . . . [plays scale on metallophone].

David:	Let's practice our scales. Sing along with me [sings scale using syllable "la"]!
David:	Musicians often will put words to the scale to help them remember the sound of the notes. So they'll sing "do-re-mi-fa-sol-la-ti-do." Try that [the musicians and audience sing]. Once again.
David:	Now, to do it fast, it helps to practice small parts of it fast. Repeat after me: do-re-mi!
Audience:	Do-re-mi!
David:	Do-re-mi!
Audience:	Do-re-mi!
David:	Mi-fa-sol!
Audience:	Mi-fa-sol!
David:	Fa-sol-la!
Audience:	Fa-sol-la!
David:	La-ti-do!
Audience:	La-ti-do!
David:	Do-re-mi-fa!
Audience:	Do-re-mi-fa!
David:	Fa-sol-la-ti!
Audience:	Fa-sol-la-ti!
David (**slightly slower**):	Do-re-mi-fa-sol-la-ti-do!
All:	Do-re-mi-fa-sol-la-ti-do!
David:	Good! Mozart must have practiced scales a lot because he uses them all the time, and sometimes, they're about ten times faster than what we just did. But the thing that makes Mozart great is that instead of always playing—

[MUSICIANS PLAY A ONE-OCTAVE ASCENDING SCALE]

| David: | he changes the scale in some small way to make it fancy and more fun. For example, instead of just going up and down, sometimes, he might skip notes and make the music feel like it jumps around. |

[ROBERTO AND ANDRES DEMONSTRATE A SCALE IN BROKEN THIRDS]

| David: | Or, he'll put little decorations called ornaments on certain notes of a scale. |

[SOOVIN DEMONSTRATES A SCALE WITH TURNS AND APPOGIATURAS]

| David: | Or he might have lots of stuff going on around a scale. |

[PHILIP DEMONSTRATES A SCALE THAT PIVOTS AROUND A TONIC PEDAL]

| David: | Now the musicians are going to play more of the piece we heard at the beginning, the Piano Quartet in Eb. This time, let's notice all of Mozart's beautiful scales. Some of them will be normal; some will be decorated; some will have lots of things happening around them. Let's listen! |

[MUSICIANS PERFORM III. *ALLEGRETTO,* PICK UPS TO BAR 256 TO THE END]

David: So Mozart was great at playing scales, and he made them interesting by changing them up. As you heard, sometimes he even turned a simple scale into a beautiful melody—that's another reason people think Mozart was a great composer; he wrote wonderful tunes. He was great at writing beautiful melodies that are very easy to sing and very easy to remember. The next piece has a melody that is so clear and beautiful that you'll never forget it. Marya, play the melody for us.

[MARYA PLAYS BARS 1–8 OF FLUTE QUARTET IN D MAJOR, K. 285, III. RONDO]

David: That's a lovely melody, and it's easy to remember. Marya, could you play that again, a little slower and let us hum along with it?

[MARYA PLAYS THE MELODY THREE MORE TIMES, GRADUALLY WORKING UP TO TEMPO AS DAVID AND THE AUDIENCE HUM AND PLAY IMAGINARY FLUTES]

David: We're lucky because we get to hear that melody many times because this next piece is a rondo. How many of you were here last week? Can any of you tell me how a rondo pattern works? . . . Yes, in the black shirt!

Child #5: A rondo is when there's something that is the main thing that comes back. And there's more that happens in between. So [you hear it] at the beginning, then in the middle a couple of times, and at the end.

[AUDIENCE APPLAUDS]

David: Excellent! Just for that, you're going to be one of my rondo volunteers! So a rondo is a piece of music where you hear the tune, then you hear something different; you hear the tune again, then you hear something different, and so on. The musicians had so much fun making a rondo together with you last week that we're going to do it again, only today instead of using Brahms's gypsy violin music, we're going to use Mozart's flute music.

  In our rondo, the musicians are going to start with Mozart's flute theme then . . . what's your name?

Child #5: Ariel.

David: Then, Ariel is going to play some scales on the metallophone. You can make them plain or fancy; it's up to you. Then, if this is a rondo, who's going to play next?

Audience: The musicians!

David: Let's all sing a song. Does anybody have a birthday today?

Child #6 (raising hand): I do!

David: Really? What's your name?

Child #6: David.

David: Good name! So we'll all sing "Happy Birthday" to David, and then if this is a rondo, who plays next?

Audience: The musicians!

David: Right! And since Mozart liked energetic rhythms, I'd like another volunteer to play a rhythmic drum solo . . . yes, in the orange coveralls!

David: So our rondo will go musicians, metallophone scales, musicians, "Happy Birthday," musicians, drum, musicians.

[CREATE A RONDO WITH THE A SECTION OF THE MOZART AND AUDIENCE EPISODES. MUSICIANS ACCOMPANY THE SONG]

David: Fantastic! Now we're going to hear Mozart's rondo for flute quartet, and you'll get to hear what he decided to write instead of "Happy Birthday" or music for drums or metallophone. And to show me that you remember that melody . . . how's it go? Can you hum it for me? [audience hums melody with David] Every time you hear that memorable flute melody, get your imaginary flute out and play along. Let's hear Mozart's rondo!

[MUSICIANS PERFORM RONDO]

David: One more thing that was really great about Mozart is that he wrote wonderful songs and terrific operas. Who can tell me what an opera is?

Child #7: It's like a play in which everyone sings.

David: Very good. A play in which everyone sings. So it's like a story that is sung and acted out instead of just read. Actually, a good friend of mine was just in an opera of a story you probably know—*Green Eggs and Ham*! Last year a composer named Robert Kapilow turned *Green Eggs and Ham* into an opera, so people were walking onstage singing [sung] "I do not like green eggs and ham! I do not like them, Sam I Am!"

Just for fun, let's make up a little bit of opera! The musicians have some chords you might hear in a Mozart opera, and we're going make up our own opera. Who here would like to be an opera star? [volunteers come forward] Marya, do you want to be an opera star?

Marya: Sure! Why not!

David: Okay, so I'll get us started, and when I bring this microphone to you, you'll sing what comes next. We're going to make up a story—we don't know what it's going to be about, but we'll figure it out! Ready, musicians?

[PIANO QUARTET SUSTAINS THE FIRST NOTE OF THE MOZART RE-CITATIVE PROGRESSION AND CHANGES TO THE NEXT CHORDS ON DAVID'S CUE]

David (singing): Once upon a time, there was a—
Child #8: fox . . . that had a fluffy tail.
David: Once upon a time, there was a fox that had a fluffy tail. And then one day the fox with the fluffy tail met a—
Child #9: cat.
David: A cat who liked to—
Child #9: sing
David: in a very high-pitched voice, and this is what the cat sang—
Child #10: LAAAAAAA!!!!!!!!!!!
David: One day the cat turned to the fox and said—
Child #11: hi!
David: And the fox answered—
Child #12: hi!
Marya: Then the fox said, "I'm going to eat you up!" Oh, no! What shall we do? Shall we run through the forest? Should we go quickly now?
David: But then the fox said, "You know, I don't really like eating cats, especially singing cats, so why don't we just have a tea party and call it quits?" And they lived happily ever after!

[LAUGHTER AND APPLAUSE]

David: Thank you! Let's have a hand for our opera stars! Okay, that was a pretty silly opera—the opera of the fox and the cat, but you know, that's just as silly as a lot of Mozart operas. One of my favorite Mozart operas is called *The Magic Flute*. How many of you know what you want to be when you grow up? Do any of you want to be a birdcatcher when you grow up? In *The Magic Flute*, there's a birdcatcher, and his name is Papageno. He catches birds and sells their feathers for hats and things like that. Papageno is a pretty happy birdcatcher, but he's also a little lonely because he really wants a wife, and he doesn't have one. He sings a song where he says, "You know, I'd give my best feather if I could just find a wife, and we'd be as happy as two turtledoves"—a turtledove is kind of like a pigeon. Let's learn this song. Listen to me sing it first; if you know the song and can read the words, you can join in, too.

[PHILIP BUSH PLAYS INTRODUCTION AND ACCOMPANIMENT. MUSICIANS ADD IN.]

David: "I'd give my finest feather to find a pretty wife! / Two turtle doves together / We'd share a happy life! / We'd share a happy life! / We'd share a happy life!"

Now, obviously I'm no opera star, but it's fun to pretend I am sometimes, so I'm going to sing this again, but this time, I'd like you to sing with me. First, let's learn the words. Let's get a beat going.

[AUDIENCE PATS A BEAT AND LEARNS THE LYRICS THROUGH A CALL AND RESPONSE CHANT IN MOZART'S RHYTHM]

David: Ready to sing? Phil's going to give us an introduction, then we'll come in.

[EVERYONE SINGS THE PAPAGENO SONG]

David: Mozart was not only a great writer of operas and songs, but sometimes he would also take a song and write a theme and variations on it. What does that mean? It means you take the song and play it with different flavors. Who here likes ice cream? Let's name some different flavors of ice cream—

Child #13:   Strawberry!

Child #14:   Mint chocolate chip!

Child #15:   Vanilla!

Child #16:   Cherry!

David: So we just named four flavors of ice cream, and we could probably keep going until we named fifty different varieties. Mozart was such a good composer that he easily could have composed fifty different variations or flavors of the Papageno song. Could we hear what it might sound like if Papageno were a very depressed birdcatcher instead of a happy birdcatcher?

[MUSICIANS IMPROVISE A SOMBER MINOR VARIATION]

David: Wow. You can hear that's an entirely different flavor. Who can suggest a way they can change the Papageno song to make another variation? What do you think?

Child #17:   Make it faster.

David: Faster! Let's hear a super-fast version of the Papageno song!

[MUSICIANS PLAY AN ALLEGRO VERSION]

David: One more idea; what could they do?

Child #18:   I want it slow, but very, very happy!

David: Slow, but very, very happy. So maybe Papageno is deeply in love here.

[MUSICIANS IMPROVISE A SLOW, HIGHLY ORNAMENTED VERSION
WITH TRILLS AND SCALES]

David: Mozart would create variations on tunes, just like you did.
             And other composers have been inspired by Mozart's music
             and have written variations on it. You see, that's actually
             one of the greatest things about Mozart—his music still gives
             composers ideas and models for writing great music.

             Beethoven wrote some variations for cello and piano
             based on the Papageno song, but right now, we're going to
             hear a piano trio—Soovin, Andres, and Phil. They're going
             to play some variations on the Papageno song by a living
             composer Paul Reale, who lives in California.

             The first variation starts out lighthearted and highly
             decorated, like the variation you just created. Then, you'll hear
             a very angry version, like maybe it's Papageno on a very bad
             day. It's rough and dark sounding. Finally there's going to be
             a fun, jazzy variation. So maybe it's how the Papageno song
             might sound if Mozart had lived long enough to hear jazz. As
             you listen to these variations, you'll hear scales, great melodies
             that you remember, and ideas that are just as fun as the ones
             we just heard.

[MUSICIANS PLAY REALE, CUTTING FROM BAR 52 (4 AFTER B) TO LET-
TER J (BAR 134), THEN PLAY TO THE END]

David: Okay, so who remembers one of the things that make Mozart
             great?
Child #19:   He was a great musician.
David: Good. What else?
Child #20:   He did lots of themes and variations and was good at it.
Child #21:   He was a great composer.
David: Let's ask the musicians what they think makes Mozart great.
             Soovin what do you think?

[MUSICIANS RESPOND FREELY]

Soovin: He writes really beautiful melodies.
David: Phil, what do you think?
Phil: I think he's great because no matter how many times you play
             his music, you keep finding new things in it. You never get
             tired of it.
David: What about you Roberto?
Roberto: He *loved* the viola!
David: That's true! Some of the best viola music is Mozart.
Andres (**challenging his brother**): I thought he loved the cello!
Roberto: No!
David: Marya—did he love the flute?

Marya: Well, rumor has it that he hated the flute! It's true! He wrote a letter to his father when he was about twenty-eight years old because this man named Wendling had commissioned him to write three flute quartets, one of which we played today. And Mozart was so mad that he had to write these flute quartets because actually interested in a young woman, and he'd rather be spending time with her. So he wrote, "Confound it! I've got to stay at home and write these quartets for such an ugly instrument!"

David: But if he really thought it was an ugly instrument, how did he make it sound so beautiful? He must not have really meant it. What do you think makes Mozart great, Marya?

Marya: There's so much life in his music. Even in the way he'll take something as simple as a scale and change it into something wonderful.

David: Well, if you think Mozart's great, we're performing an all-Mozart chamber music concert tomorrow night at 7:00. And as a special treat, an actor will be reading letters Mozart wrote around the time each piece was composed. So we'll hope to see you there! Let's have one more round of applause for today's truly great musicians!

The Secrets of Chamber Music

*T*he *Secrets of Chamber Music* is another Kids' Concert designed for the Bridge-hampton Chamber Music Festival. (See the introduction to *What's So Great about Mozart?* for a synopsis of the context and venue.)

The festival's artistic director Marya Martin and I decided that it would be wonderful to offer a concert teaching children what chamber music is and how to listen to it. And like Leonard Bernstein's *Young People's Concerts*, we wanted to produce a concert where the parents could learn something as well.

Since the busy festival schedule allowed for only one rehearsal, most of the repertoire was culled from music the musicians were performing on the series of evening concerts. From the repertoire, I devised a list of seven "secrets" about chamber music, which the audience would discover as the evening progressed.

I commissioned artist Stacy Beam to create a poster illustrating the seven secrets, but going the extra mile, he created seven amazing and humorous paint-ings. Each painting was uncovered as the audience discovered a secret, and I was able to refer to these illustrations throughout.

The powerful notion of secrets actually came from a punning title that hit me out of the blue: *Harry Potter and the Secrets of Chamber Music*. I considered this catchy theme, but after a little reading and research (I knew nothing about the books at the time), I realized there was no way I could create a Harry Potter concert that would satisfy diehard fans while meeting our musical agenda. But the detour gave me a clever activity idea, as you'll see.

Special thanks to Uli Speth of the Diller-Quaille String Quartet for the noo-dle entry point and to the Teaching Artists of the New York Philharmonic for the "go" game!

The Secrets of Chamber Music: A Family Concert for the Bridgehampton Chamber Music Festival

Marya Martin, flute
Scott St. John, violin
Todd Phillips, violin
Cynthia Phelps, viola
John Sharp, cello

Joyce Yang, piano
David Wallace, host and arranger

Program:
    W. A. Mozart: Exposition to Piano Sonata in C Major, K. 545
    W. A. Mozart: Exposition of Piano Sonata in C Major, K. 545 arranged as
a piece of chamber music
    W. A. Mozart: String Quartet in F Major, K. 590, IV. Allegro
    W. A. Mozart: 12 Piano Variations on "Ah, vous dirai-je, Maman?"

    Theme, right hand only
    Theme, both hands
    Variation 4
    Variation 12

    W. A. Mozart: Flute Quartet in D Major, K. 285, II. Adagio
    W. A. Mozart: Excerpt: Flute Quartet in D Major, K. 285, II. Adagio
arranged for flute and piano
    Felix Mendelssohn: Piano Trio in D Minor, Op. 49, I. Molto Allegro ed
Agitato
    Antonin Dvorak: Piano Quintet in A Major, Op. 81, III. Molto Vivace:
Furiant

Materials:
    Telescoping pointer
    The Seven Secrets of Chamber Music paintings by artist and children's
illustrator, Stacy Wallace Beam, propped on music stands, arranged in a semicircle
at the base of the stage. Painting side is facing away, so the audience just sees the
back, which reads "Secret #1," "Secret #2," etc. Paintings are turned around as
the audience discovers each secret.
    Magic K. 545 painting by Stacy Beam is displayed center stage; black and
white side facing audience.
    The Handy-Dandy Chamber-Music-Converter Box—a gigantic, cardboard
case binding, covered in silver wrapping paper.

[MUSICIANS ENTER. JOYCE YANG PERFORMS EXPOSITION OF
MOZART'S PIANO SONATA IN C MAJOR, K. 545.]

David: Good afternoon, and welcome to today's concert! How many
of you know a secret? [show of hands] How many of you like
to be told a secret that not everyone else knows? [larger show
of hands] Well, have we got a concert for you, because today,
you're going to learn seven big secrets about chamber music—
what it is and how to listen to it, plus, we'll discover a lot more
little secrets along the way.
    A moment ago we just heard our wonderful pianist Joyce
Yang play the beginning of a piano sonata by Mozart; I've got
the music right here.

[GESTURE TO THE *MAGIC K. 545* PAINTING WHICH IS AN ENLARGED, BLACK AND WHITE DEPICTION OF THE FIRST TWO SYSTEMS OF THE PIANO SONATA.]

David: Raise your hand if you think that might be a piece of chamber music.
            Raise your hand if you think it might not a piece of chamber music.
            Raise your hand if you have *no idea* whether it's a piece of chamber music or not.
            Well, Joyce, is that sonata a piece of chamber music?
Joyce: Nope!
David: No? That's too bad, because I came here to hear some chamber music—but I'll tell you what—I brought my Handy-Dandy Chamber Music Converter Box, so we're going to turn this piece of solo piano music into a piece of chamber music.

[PUTS THE *MAGIC K. 545* PAINTING INTO THE "CONVERTER BOX"]

David: I'm going to put this music in this box, twirl it around, and at the count of three, we'll say the secret chamber music words: "Neue Mozart Ausgabe!"[1] Let's try those words—
All: Neue . . . Mozart . . . Ausgabe!
David: Okay, ready? One! . . . Two! . . . Three! . . .
All: **Neue Mozart Ausgabe!**

[DAVID SPINS THE CONVERTER BOX WITH EACH WORD, THEN OPENS IT TO REVEAL THE OPPOSITE SIDE OF THE *MAGIC K. 545* PAINTING, WHICH IS A MULTICOLORED SCORE OF THE FIRST SYSTEM OF DAVID'S SEXTET ARRANGEMENT]

David: Now it's a piece of chamber music! Let's listen to it and hear what's different.

[SEXTET PERFORMS K. 545 ARRANGEMENT]

David: So what happened? Who can raise a hand and tell me something that was different now that it's a piece of chamber music?
Child #1:   The whole band is playing instead of just the piano!
David: Very good! You have just discovered Secret #1: Chamber music has to have at least two musicians playing music together.

[DAVID TURNS AROUND SECRET #1 TO REVEAL A PAINTING OF FIVE MUSICIANS JOYFULLY PLAYING TOGETHER WHILE IN THE BACKGROUND, A LONE PIANIST SITS PRACTICING AN ETUDE]

David [pointing to painting]: One guy playing piano all by himself is playing solo. He needs at least one more person to play with

---

[1] German for "New Mozart edition"; the official title of Bärenreiter's esteemed Urtext edition. In addition to providing a fun phrase, these words provided a surprise inside joke for the benefit of the musicians onstage and in the audience.

	him to be making chamber music. Now, Todd Phillips, one of our violinists today, plays in a group called The Orpheus Chamber Orchestra. That's an orchestra that makes chamber music. Todd, how many musicians can be playing in the Orpheus Chamber Orchestra?
Todd:	Oh, we can have like twenty-six, thirty, even up to thirty-five sometimes.
David:	So you can have as many as thirty-five people playing chamber music?
Todd:	Absolutely.
David:	Cynthia Phelps, our violist, is principal violist of the New York Philharmonic, and John Sharp, our cellist, is principal cellist of the Chicago Symphony. When we see the New York Philharmonic or the Chicago Symphony, we have more than two people. Are we hearing chamber music?
Cynthia:	That would be no.

[LAUGHTER]

David:	No? Why not?
Cynthia:	Well, there's about a hundred people and they play orchestral music, which is a lot bigger than chamber music.
John:	We also have someone who stands in front of us and waves a baton.
David:	Does anyone know what that person is called?
Child #2:	A conductor.
David:	That's right. And we've just discovered Secret #2: Chamber music has no conductor.

[DAVID TURNS OVER SECRET NO. 2 TO REVEAL A PAINTING OF A STRING QUARTET LAUGHING AND PLAYING. IN FRONT OF THEM IS A PODIUM WITH A FEW CRUMPLED PIECES OF SHEET MUSIC AND A BROKEN BATON. THE VIOLIST IS POINTING TO THE RIGHT WHERE THE VIEWER SEES THE RIGHT FOOT AND THE TAILS OF THE EXITING CONDUCTOR.]

David:	You can see that it looks like somebody tried to conduct this string quartet, but he broke his baton and left! Chamber musicians don't need a conductor. They play by themselves with no one else to show them how fast to play, how soft or loud to be, or when to start or stop. Chamber musicians are very proud of being able to do that. But I think there must be some secrets they're not telling us, because I don't know how as many as thirty-five people can play together without having a conductor! I want us to try and figure out how they're playing together.
	When I say "Go!" I want everybody to start clapping. BUT, I want us to end up clapping the same beat. If we can do

that, maybe you can tell me how we managed to do it. Alright? Ready? GO!

[AUDIENCE CLAPS AND ESTABLISHES A BEAT WITHIN ABOUT THREE SECONDS]

David: Excellent! How did you do that?

Child #3: We adjusted.

David: Do you guys adjust when you're playing chamber music?

Musicians: All the time! Oh, yes!

David: What else did we do to get together?

Child #4: We followed beats.

David: Whose beat were you following?

Child #4: My own.

David: But how did you get everybody else to be with *you*?

Child #4: I don't know.

David: Does anybody else have an idea how we ended up with him?

Child #5: We did it by recognizing that everybody had a beat; then we used it as our own.

David: So by paying attention to everybody else's rhythm and then using it as your own. Do you do that in chamber music?

Musicians: Yeah! Yes!

David: What else?

Child #6: We listened to the people around us clapping and looked to see that we were clapping at the same time.

David: So you listened and you watched. Chamber musicians definitely have to listen, but they also use a bit of body language to stay together. Scott, could you show us a little bit about how musicians cue each other?

Scott: It's kind of like a mini-conducting kind of thing. I use my violin to show the tempo quickly by going "four-one!" [lifts violin and lowers it]

David: Let's try that. Everyone pretend like you're playing a violin and just go "four-one." Kind of "up-down." One-two-three-FOUR-ONE. Good; again. One-two-three-FOUR-ONE. Let's watch them play a passage where they have to watch and cue each other in order to be together. This is from a Mozart String Quartet.

[STRING QUARTET DEMONSTRATES EXCERPT FROM FINALE OF MOZART'S STRING QUARTET IN F MAJOR, K. 590: FROM AFTER THE FIRST FERMATA IN BAR 42 UNTIL THE F MAJOR CADENCE AFTER THE THIRD FERMATA (BAR 51 DOWNBEAT).]

David: So you could see them watching and moving together. I could even hear them breathing together. So now you know the secret of how chamber musicians play together—and chamber music is *all* about playing together! Speaking of playing together, what's the difference between playing by yourself and playing with a friend or a brother or sister?

Child #7:   Sometimes when you're playing by yourself you get kind of lonely.

David: Hmm . . . does that ever happen to you chamber musicians?

Musicians (laughing):   Yeah. Sometimes.

David: I see Joyce is shaking her head! So musicians like doing both, yes?

Child #8:   When you play by yourself, you get all the attention.

David: That's true! If you play with others, then you have to share the attention. Yes?

Child #9:   You have to share.

David: Now *that's* a very important thing that I want to explore a little bit. Chamber musicians have to share. That's Secret #3: Chamber music is all about sharing musical ideas.

[DAVID TURNS AROUND SECRET #3 PAINTING, WHICH REVEALS A STRING QUARTET WITH PATTERNS OF MULTICOLORED NOTES PASSING FROM ONE INSTRUMENT TO THE OTHER.

DAVID POINTS TO PAINTING, MUSICIANS UNDERSCORE WITH MOZART'S "NOODLE THEME" (THE PICKUP TO BAR 5 UNTIL THE DOWNBEAT OF BAR 8) AT THE APPROPRIATE TIME]

David (pointing to painting):   Often a violin will start an idea—

[SCOTT UNDERSCORES WITH MOZART'S "NOODLE" THEME]

David: Then it will pass to another instrument

[TODD UNDERSCORES WITH MOZART'S "NOODLE" THEME]

David: and to another

[CINDY UNDERSCORES WITH MOZART'S "NOODLE" THEME]

David: and another

[JOHN UNDERSCORES WITH THE MOZART'S "NOODLE" THEME]

David: It can be fun to share things you like. What are some things you like to share?

Child #10: Love.

David: That's a good thing to share. What else?

Child #11: Toys!

David: That's good, too. Musicians particularly like sharing food. How many of you like pasta like spaghetti or ravioli? Well, in the piece of chamber music you're about to hear, the musicians share a melody that reminds me of one of those spiral noodles that curls round and round. Scott could you play us that noodle melody?

[SCOTT PLAYS NOODLE MELODY.]

David: Scott's going to play that again, and let's trace the shape of that noodle in the air. Ready?

[SCOTT PLAYS THEME AGAIN; AUDIENCE TRACES THE SHAPE IN THE AIR BY DRAWING LOOPS WITH THEIR INDEX FINGERS]

David: He's going to do it one more time, and this time, let's try to sing along with him.

Scott: Three-four!

[SCOTT PLAYS, AUDIENCE GESTURES AND SINGS]

David: Let's hear a part where they pass the noodles around. The noodles will start with John, who will pass it to Cynthia, who will pass it to Todd, who will pass it to Scott. Let's hear them share the noodles!

[QUARTET PLAYS FROM AFTER THE FERMATA IN BAR 100 UNTIL THE DOWNBEAT OF BAR 105]

David: Excellent! So let's hear one of my favorite pieces of chamber music—the finale from the string quartet in F major by Wolfgang Amadeus Mozart. The secret of listening to this piece is to follow the noodles—watch to see who has the noodles and listen to how they share them!

[MUSICIANS PERFORM FINALE OF MOZART'S STRING QUARTET IN F MAJOR, K. 590]

David: That was a lot of noodles! Which musician do you think got the most noodles? I'm going to point to each musician, and when I point to the one you think played the most noodles, make your "noodle motion" in the air. Scott, it looks like you got the most noodles.

Scott: Yeah, I guess I did. Sometimes first violinists hog all the melodies; it's kind of our job!

David: Ah. You all know that when you play together with other friends, you often play different roles. Like when you play "Hide and Seek," somebody is "it," and everybody else hides; or in tag, the person who's "it" chases, and everyone else runs away.

            When you're playing chamber music, often one person is "it." They're playing one kind of music called the melody, and everybody else plays something different called the accompaniment. That's the fourth secret.

[DAVID TURNS AROUND SECRET #4, A PICTURE OF A FLUTE QUARTET WHERE STARS ARE COMING OUT OF THE STRINGED INSTRUMENTS AND A MOON IS RISING OUT OF THE FLUTE]

David: You can see in this picture, the flute is playing one kind of music that sounds like a beautiful sky with the moon and the clouds, and the strings are playing something that sounds like a bunch of stars. So she's playing the melody, and these guys are doing the accompaniment. Joyce is going to help us understand a little better what melody and accompaniment is all about. Joyce, could you play us the melody of Mozart's 12 variations on "Ah, vous dirai-je, Maman?"

[JOYCE PLAYS THE THEME WITH THE RIGHT HAND ONLY. AUDIENCE IMMEDIATELY RECOGNIZES IT AS "TWINKLE, TWINKLE, LITTLE STAR."]

David: I see a lot of you started singing along; that's the same melody as "Twinkle, Twinkle, Little Star." Now, she's going to play us the accompaniment; let's hear what that sounds like.

[JOYCE PLAYS THE LEFT HAND OF THE THEME]

David: I noticed that none of you sang along that time. That might not be a good tune for singing, but listen to what it sounds like when you have both at the same time—it's like a beautiful sky where you have both the moon and the stars.

[JOYCE PLAYS THE THEME WITH BOTH HANDS]

David: Now that's a pretty simple way to accompany a melody. Sometimes, especially in chamber music, the accompaniment becomes very complicated. Could you show us a more complicated one?

[JOYCE PERFORMS VARIATION 4]

David: And sometimes in music, the accompaniment gets so interesting and exciting that the composer decides to let the accompaniment practically take over the melody. Joyce, play us the last variation of that piece.

[JOYCE PERFORMS VARIATION 12]

David: Wow! That was really something. So was that chamber music?

Audience: No.

David: No? Are you sure? I didn't see any conductor, it sounded like her hands were sharing noodles—there was a melody and an accompaniment. Are you sure it isn't it chamber music?

Child #12: You have to have more than one person.

David: Oh, yeah. I guess you're right. Well, I'll tell you what; let's turn this into a piece of chamber music too. If you're on this half of the church, you're going to sing the melody. If you're on this side, you're going make the accompaniment. Tap one finger.

[DAVID STARTS A BEAT OF FINGER TAPPING, AND GETS TAPPERS TO WHISPER THE WORD "TWINKLE" OVER AND OVER. THE OTHER SIDE IS CUED TO BEGIN SINGING. MUSICIANS JOIN IN WITH IMPROVISED ACCOMPANIMENT. ACTIVITY IS REPEATED, SWITCHING ROLES.]

David: Wonderful. How many people are here today?

Marya: About two hundred.

David: I think we just set a world record with the world's largest piece of chamber music! Next we're going to hear a beautiful piece of chamber music where Marya, our flutist, is going to play the melody and the strings are going to accompany her. Here's the second movement of the Mozart's Flute Quartet in D Major.

[MUSICIANS PERFORM MOZART'S FLUTE QUARTET IN D MAJOR, K. 285, II. ADAGIO.]

David: So you could hear that Marya was "it." She was doing the melody and everybody else was doing the accompaniment. By the way, before they played, when we were doing melody and accompaniment, what was it like to do melody or accompaniment? How was it different?

Child #13: The accompaniment was easier.

David: Raise your hand if you thought it was easier to do the accompaniment, the tapping. Raise your hand if you thought it was easier to do the melody. Raise your hand if you thought it was more fun to do the accompaniment. Raise your hand if you thought it was more fun to do the melody . . . interesting . . . lots of different opinions. Let's poll the musicians on stage: How many of you prefer melody? How many of you like doing both? Ah, looks like the low strings like doing both, which is good, because in their role, they often end up doing both.

David: Now, here's a chamber secret that most people don't know.

[DAVID TURNS OVER SECRET #5, WHICH SHOWS A FLUTE, VIOLIN, AND CELLO ENSEMBLE WITH A TRIO SCORE EMERGING IN THE AIR FROM THEIR INSTRUMENTS. TO THEIR RIGHT, IS A FLUTIST AND PIANIST, WITH THE SAME SCORE EMERGING FROM THEIR INSTRUMENTS.]

David: In the early days of chamber music, composers would often take a popular chamber music piece and arrange it for different instrument combinations so that more people could play the piece and composers could sell more music. Back in those days, people didn't have radios or CD players. The only way to hear music was to play it yourself or to get somebody else to play it. If you wanted to hear this flute quartet, but you lived in a village where you only had a flute and a piano, you were out of luck! To solve this problem—and make more money—composers made arrangements for different instrument combinations. Did any of you hear the Beethoven Septet that we performed last Sunday? Beethoven and his publishers created many different arrangements of that piece because it was so popular. Let's hear what this quartet movement would sound like if Mozart had arranged it for flute and piano!

[NINETY-SECOND EXCERPT OF FLUTE QUARTET ARRANGED FOR FLUTE AND PIANO]

David:	So, let's see if that was chamber music. Were there at least two people?
Audience:	Yes.
David:	Was there a conductor?
Audience:	No.
David:	Did they share music together?
Audience:	Yes.
David:	Was there melody and accompaniment?
Audience:	Yes.
David:	And we just talked about this one—not all chamber music has to have arrangements, but this one does. So, what's the verdict? Is this chamber music?
Audience:	Yes!
David:	Good. Give yourselves a hand. The next secret I'm going to tell you about is probably the most important secret you're going to learn today because it's about YOU. It's a secret about what makes a good chamber music listener. I didn't figure out this secret until I was almost a grown-up, so listen carefully.

[DAVID TURNS OVER SECRET #6, A PAINTING OF A THOUGHTFUL PERSON WITH VARIOUS INSTRUMENTS ARRAYED AROUND HIS HEAD IN A THOUGHT BUBBLE]

David:	The secret is this: a good chamber music listener listens for who is "it." That means noticing when the musicians switch from playing melody to playing accompaniment. In the last two pieces of music, the flute always had the melody and never had accompaniment, but in most chamber music, the musicians take turns playing the melody. It's like a game of tag where one person has the melody, then they tag someone else and they have the melody.
	Unlike the noodle piece we heard earlier, often the melody keeps changing. But the good thing is, it's usually slower and smoother than the accompaniment, so it's not too hard to tell which is which. A good chamber musician or listener listens to hear, "Okay . . . now the violin has the melody . . . now it passes to the cello . . . and then to the piano."

We're going to hear some of Felix Mendelssohn's Trio in D minor, Op. 49, and the melody changes from person to person a lot, but it's usually slower and smoother, so it's easy to follow. It will begin with the cello—John, could you play us the opening, please?

[JOHN PLAYS OPENING PHRASE]

David: Then it's like he tags Scott and Scott has the melody.

[SCOTT PLAYS HIS FIRST MELODY]

David: And of course, Joyce gets a turn, and there will be times when more than one person is playing melody together. Let's listen to see if we can follow who is "it"; who has the melody.

[TRIO PERFORMS THE EXPOSITION OF THE FIRST MOVEMENT OF MENDELSSOHN'S PIANO TRIO IN D MINOR, OP. 49]

David: We have one piece left to play for you, and we have one last secret—but it's really not that big of a secret by now.

[DAVID TURNS OVER SECRET #7, A PAINTING OF THE PIANO QUINTET PLAYING AND IMMENSELY ENJOYING THEMSELVES]

David: Playing chamber music is fun! That's why every chamber musician thinks chamber music is the best music in the whole world! So the musicians are going to play one last piece; it's the Furiant from the Piano Quintet in A major by Antonin Dvorak. When they're finished, you're going to tell me whether it's chamber music, and why or why not. But before we do, let's review some of the secrets of chamber music. What's one?

Child #14: Chamber music has got to be more than one person.

Child #15: There can't be a conductor.

Child #16: People share the music.

Child #17: There's a harmony and a melody.

David: Good. A harmony and melody, or melody and accompaniment.

Child #18: It has to flow between people.

Child #19: A good chamber music person always knows who has the melody.

David: Yes, in the pink?

Child #20: Play tag!

David: What?

Child #20: Play tag!

David: Yes, it's like they play tag and pass the melody off. So the musicians are going to play this quintet, and I want you to watch and listen to see how many secrets you notice. At the end, we'll see if it fits the definition of chamber music.

[MUSICIANS PERFORM DVORAK: PIANO QUINTET IN A MAJOR, OP. 81, III. MOLTO VIVACE: FURIANT, COMPLETE.]

David:	Okay, let's test this quintet against the secrets of chamber music. Were there at least two people?
Audience:	Yes!
David:	Was there a conductor?
Audience:	No!
David:	Were they sharing musical ideas?
Audience:	Yes!
David:	Did you hear melody and accompaniment?
Audience:	Yes!
David:	Chamber music doesn't have to be an arrangement, so we can skip this picture, but what about this one—were you a good chamber music listener?
Audience:	Yes!
David:	And was that fun?
Audience:	Yes! [applause]
David:	And it was especially fun because they're some of the best chamber musicians in the world! Let's have them take a bow as we give them one more big round of applause!

Myths and Legends

*M*yths and Legends is an orchestral interactive concert created for the Hudson Valley Philharmonic Orchestra, a regional orchestra with an extensive educational outreach program under the auspices of the Bardavon 1869 Opera House. The concert was designed for target audiences of approximately 800 to 1,200 students ranging in age from eight to twelve. (Most audiences included older and younger members as well.) Each year's program is performed twelve to fourteen times at the Bardavon 1869 Opera House and high school auditoriums in the region.

All participating schools received a Teachers' Guide with preparatory and follow-up activities, and many schools received visits from HVP Teaching Artists and touring ensembles. As part of the visits for *Myths and Legends*, the musicians helped students to compose a new work that was premiered at the orchestral concert. I jointly created the script with conductor Marietta Cheng, producer Chris Silva, and actor Russell G. Jones.

One aspect of the Hudson Valley Philharmonic concerts that always requires a bit of finesse is the concerto. Every year, the concert features the winner of a concerto competition, and (in the immortal words of Forrest Gump), you never know what you're going to get. We may be leading a program about American music, but halfway through the concert, we must include the Bruch g minor Violin Concerto. If you find yourself in a similar situation, don't despair; a connection can always be made, whether conceptual, musical, or contextual. However, it's up to you to make the connection; don't leave your audience wondering how a piece fits in with your through-line.

Myths and Legends: A Concert for the Hudson Valley Philharmonic's Classroom to Concert Program

Marietta Cheng, conductor
Russell G. Jones, actor and Teaching Artist
David Wallace, musician and Teaching Artist
Kay Churchill, director of education
Chris Silva, producer and director

Program:
> Ludwig van Beethoven: *The Creatures of Prometheus*
> Manuel de Falla: "Ritual Fire Dance" from *El Amor Brujo*
> Richard Wagner: Overture to *The Flying Dutchman*
> Children of the Hudson Valley: *Myths, Legends, and Fairy Tales*

Wolfgang Amadeus Mozart: Flute Concerto No. 2 in D Major, K.V 314

Mikhail Glinka: Overture to *Russlan and Lyudmila*

House manager gives initial welcome, which concludes "please stay in your seats following the performance until your bus is called. Thank you."

House and stage go to black. Conductor special slow fade up as Marietta enters its glow.

Perform The Creatures of Prometheus with lighting highlighting different sections according to orchestration.

[DAVID AND RUSSELL ENTER FROM THE REAR OF THE HOUSE WITH MARIETTA'S NARRATION]

Marietta (MC):	Good morning and welcome to the Bardavon 1869 Opera House! I'm Marietta Cheng, guest conductor of the Hudson Valley Philharmonic. At today's concert, we will be performing great music that was inspired by stories that are larger than life—fairytales, myths, and legends. Two friends of mine will help us explore how the orchestra can tell these stories through music. Please welcome Russell G. Jones and David Wallace!
Russell (RJ):	Good morning! I'm Russell G. Jones, actor and Teaching Artist.
David (DW):	And I'm David Wallace, musician and Teaching Artist. We just heard *The Creatures of Prometheus* by Ludwig van Beethoven.
RJ:	The Prometheus myth is an ancient Greek tale that goes back thousands of years. According to this story, at the beginning of time, two giants named Epimetheus and Prometheus modeled all the people and animals of the earth out of clay. [gestures the fashioning of creatures] When they had finished sculpting all the creatures, they breathed on them, and they came alive!
DW:	According to the myth, Prometheus gave humans the gift of fire.
RJ (interjecting):	Now, wait a minute—I could see how those fast violin notes could demonstrate birds flying or animals hopping around, but I don't think I heard anything that reminded me of fire. Did you? Marietta, *can* composers write fiery sounding music for the orchestra?
MC:	Well, actually, Russell, the next piece we want to play is "Ritual Fire Dance" from a ballet called *El Amor Brujo* (Love the Magician). This ballet by Spanish composer Manuel de Falla is based on a gypsy ghost legend. Not only does the music sound fiery at times, but the rhythm also makes you want to dance.

DW: Before we hear "Ritual Fire Dance," I think it would be fun to explore how we can get the orchestra to make some fiery sounds. You all probably know the four families of the orchestra, right? Up front, we have the strings . . .

[STRINGS FACE AUDIENCE, SMILE, AND WAVE THEIR BOWS AND PLAY THE FIRST TWO BARS OF MOZART'S *EINE KLEINE MACHTMUSIK*.]

MC: behind them are the woodwinds . . .

[WOODWINDS HOLD UP THEIR INSTRUMENTS AND PLAY WOODWIND CHORALE FROM WAGNER'S OVERTURE TO *THE FLYING DUTCHMAN*]

RJ: all the way back we have the brass . . .

[BRASS INSTRUMENTS HOLD UP THEIR INSTRUMENTS AND PLAY RICHARD WAGNER'S *FLYING DUTCHMAN* LEITMOTIF]

DW: and in the back representing percussion, we have Rick our timpanist.

[RICK PLAYS A TIMPANI SOLO]

RJ (**going into the audience with wireless mic**): Who can tell me a section you think would be good at making some fiery sounding music?

[RUSSELL TAKES TWO SUGGESTIONS. SECTION PLAYS APPROPRIATE EXCERPT FROM *EL AMOR BRUJO*. DW AFFIRMS THE CHOICES WITH COMMENTS LIKE, "YEAH, THOSE TRILLS KIND OF SOUND LIKE FLAMES LEAPING UP AND DOWN!"]

RJ: Okay, I think we're ready to hear the orchestra build a fire!
MC: I still feel like there's something missing—every fire I've seen has some crackling and popping. I think we'll have to add a fifth section to the orchestra—the audience!
RJ: So, let's see what we can do to sound like a crackling fire.

[RJ TAKES TWO OR THREE SUGGESTIONS, TRIES THEM, THEN HAS MARIETTA CHOOSE THE ONE SHE THINKS IS MOST APPROPRIATE]

RJ: Okay, now I *know* we're ready.
DW: While Marietta is conducting the orchestra, I'll be conducting you. If I point to you, that means start. If I do this it means what?
RJ (**with kids**): Louder.
DW (**whispering**): And this?
RJ (**whispering with kids**): Softer!
DW: And this?
RJ (**whispering**): Stop!
DW: Great! Watch me for your cues. Now let's build a musical fire.

[LIGHTING RESPONDS WITH APPROPRIATE EFFECTS, VARYING INTENSITY WITH THE ORCHESTRA AND AUDIENCE'S IMPROVISATION]

RJ: So imagine you're out in the forest. It's totally dark, but off in the distance, you see a flicker. [Marietta brings in orchestra] You see a fire as you get closer. The fire crackles and grows . . . [audience to add crackles] and grows . . . and the fire dies down . . . until the last ember dies and you become totally silent. [end of crackling] Totally still. You come out of the forest and back to the Bardavon 1869 Opera House [orchestra cuts off] where you silently listen to the Hudson Valley Philharmonic play Manuel de Falla's "Ritual Fire Dance."

[IMMEDIATE SEGUE TO PERFORMANCE OF "RITUAL FIRE DANCE." LIGHTING PROJECTS FLAME GOBOS AT CLIMAX]

RJ: Now *that* was fiery!

MC: So you can see how our musicians can make sounds or rhythms to help us imagine the images of a story. They also do this by playing a short melody called a leitmotif. Could everyone say *leitmotif?*

DW: A leitmotif can represent a character, an object, or an idea.

RJ: You can hear this all the time in movies.

[DOUBLE BASSES SUDDENLY INTERRUPT WITH *JAWS* THEME ON THE PITCHES E-F. LIGHTING PROJECTS A SHARK GOBO.]

RJ: The film composer John Williams used those two notes *da-nuh* to represent a shark in the movie *Jaws.* Every time you hear that leitmotif—*da-nuh! da-nuh! da-nuh da-nuh da-nuh da-nuh!*—you *know* the shark is about to attack!

[BASS INSTRUMENTS REPEAT THE LEITMOTIF AND ACCELERATE AS RJ PANTOMIMES BECOMING A SHARK AND ATTACKS DW]

DW: Well, there won't be any sharks in the next piece, but the legend behind it does involve the ocean. We're going to hear Richard Wagner's overture to *The Flying Dutchman*, an opera based on an old Norwegian legend.

RJ: Since you are such a smart audience, we want to give you a challenge. There are *four* really important leitmotifs in this overture, and each one represents something different. One represents the Flying Dutchman, another represents Senta, a young lady who wants to marry him, a third leitmotif represents some jolly Norwegian sailors, and the fourth one represents the stormy sea.

DW [enumerating on his fingers]: So that's the Flying Dutchman, Senta, the woman who wants to marry him, the Norwegian sailors, and the stormy sea.

RJ: That's right. We want to see if you can learn to recognize these leitmotifs *without our even telling you which is which*. David and I are going to tell the story in words, and the orchestra is going to help by adding in the leitmotifs.

DW: When we're done, the orchestra will play the overture to *The Flying Dutchman* for us. This is the music you would hear at the very beginning of the opera before the singing and action starts. When they're finished, Russell and I will give you a little quiz and see if you figured out the leitmotifs. Think you can do it? Okay, listen carefully. The legend of "The Flying Dutchman . . ."

RJ: Once upon a time, there was a courageous sea captain named *the Flying Dutchman*. [points to orchestra]

[ORCHESTRA PLAYS DUTCHMAN LEITMOTIF]

DW: The Flying Dutchman sailed his ship all over the world. But there was one place he could never sail past—the Cape of Good Hope at the very southern tip of Africa. He tried to sail around this cape many times, but he was always stopped by the *stormy sea*. [points to orchestra]

[ORCHESTRA PLAYS STORMY SEA LEITMOTIF]

RJ: One day, the ship captain said, "I, the Flying Dutchman, will sail around this Cape or spend forever trying!"

DW: The Devil overheard the ship captain, and said—

[SOUND PERSON ADDS DELAY AND REVERB TO RJ'S VOICE]

RJ [laughing diabolically]: Very well! You are cursed to sail forever on the *stormy sea*. But every seven years, you may go back to the shore to try and break this curse. I will end the curse if you can find a woman who will marry you and love you forever . . . but you never will! [laughs again]

DW: Many years passed, but the Flying Dutchman could never find a woman who would marry him.

RJ: One year, the Dutchman went into harbor and met a ship of *Norwegian sailors*.

[ORCHESTRA PLAYS SAILORS LEITMOTIF]

RJ: The Dutchman called to the Norwegian ship captain and offered to give him great treasure—chests full of silver, gold, and jewels—if he'd just give him a place to spend the night.

DW: The Norwegian captain saw the treasure and agreed. When they got home, they were greeted by the Norwegian captain's daughter, *Senta*.

[ORCHESTRA PLAYS SENTA/REDEMPTION LEITMOTIF]

DW: Senta had heard about the Flying Dutchman and longed to be the one to marry him and free him from his curse. And guess what? That night, the Dutchman asks Senta to marry him, and she accepts.

RJ: But wait—the story's not over yet! The Dutchman returns to the dock, where the *Norwegian sailors* are celebrating.

DW: The Dutchman is getting ready for the wedding, but Erik, an old boyfriend of Senta's, rushes onto the scene and says:

RJ: "Hey, everybody; Senta has changed her mind and agreed to marry me." [uses characterization, dialects, and ad libs for humor]

DW: The Dutchman thinks he has been betrayed and sets sail on the *stormy sea.*

RJ: Just as the ship is leaving the harbor, Senta runs out to the top of a cliff and says, "Erik is lying! I love you, Flying Dutchman! I'll be faithful forever!" She dives off the cliff into the sea! But story ends happily as the Flying Dutchman's ship rises with the Dutchman and Senta together forever.

DW: Now, let's listen for those leitmotifs as the Hudson Valley Philharmonic performs the overture to *The Flying Dutchman.*

[PERFORM OVERTURE TO *THE FLYING DUTCHMAN*]

RJ: Wow! The orchestra really did tell the whole story. I could hear the Flying Dutchman, Senta, the Norwegian sailors, and even the stormy sea. Raise your hand if you heard some of those leitmotifs as you listened.

DW: Great! Because now it's time for the challenge; see if you can tell us who this is.

[ORCHESTRA PLAYS DUTCHMAN LEITMOTIF; AUDIENCE IDENTIFIES.]

RJ: Right! The Flying Dutchman. Wagner's use of the brass instruments really helps to bring out his strength and determination.

DW: And what do these swirling scales in the strings strings represent?

[ORCHESTRA PLAYS STORMY SEA LEITMOTIF; AUDIENCE IDENTIFIES.]

DW: Right! The stormy sea.

RJ: But see if you remember who this one is.

[ORCHESTRA PLAYS SENTA LEITMOTIF; AUDIENCE IDENTIFIES.]

RJ: Senta! You're three for three!

DW: And whose leitmotif has these short, dancing notes?

[ORCHESTRA PLAYS SAILORS LEITMOTIF; AUDIENCE IDENTIFIES.]

DW: Perfect! The Norwegian sailors.

MC: Our next piece *Myths, Legends, and Fairytales*, was not
    written by Beethoven, de Falla, or Wagner. It was written
    by kids from schools in the Hudson Valley, including many
    of you.

DW: To prepare for today's concert, many of you had visits from
    Hudson Valley Philharmonic musicians who helped you
    compose music inspired by myths, fairytales, and legends.
    Participating schools included: [DW names schools du jour].
    The first section was inspired by the fairytale *Cinderella*. The
    melodies you'll hear are leitmotifs representing the characters
    Cinderella, the fairy godmother, the wicked stepmother, and
    the prince.

[ORCHESTRA PLAYS LETTER A. RJ PANTOMIMES EACH CHARACTER
ACCORDING TO THE MUSIC.]

DW: Dynamics—the loudness or softness of music—helps to give
    the music a certain mood or feeling. In the next part, students
    who were studying the Prometheus myth used loud dynamics
    to demonstrate the supernatural power of gods. They used soft
    dynamics to represent people and animals.

[ORCHESTRA PLAYS LETTER B. RJ PANTOMIMES THE PROMETHEUS
MYTH.]

DW: Of course, music doesn't always have to tell a story. The next
    music was written by students who just put together notes that
    they liked. You'll notice a nice contrast between short, staccato
    notes, and smooth legato notes.

[ORCHESTRA PLAYS LETTER C. RJ DOES AN INTERPRETIVE MODERN
DANCE.]

DW: The final section was inspired by a local legend made
    famous by the writer Washington Irving. This music was
    inspired by headless horseman from "The Legend of Sleepy
    Hollow." Notice how the galloping rhythm really creates
    excitement.

[ORCHESTRA PLAYS LETTER D. RJ PULLS HIS SHIRT OVER HIS HEAD,
PANTOMIMES THE GALLOPING HORSEMAN, LEAPS FROM THE
STAGE.]

DW: Great music, everybody! Give yourselves a hand! Just as stories
    can be larger than life, truly great people can seem larger than
    life. Often we speak of great musicians as being legends. The

Bardavon Opera House has a slogan that says "Legendary Performances since 1869." For over 135 years, people have come here to hear the best and most famous performers in the world.

MC: Today, we're going to hear the winner of this year's Virtuoso in Progress competition. That means he is one of the best young musicians in the *entire* Hudson Valley—maybe a legend in the making!

RJ: He's a senior representing Arlington High School and will be performing the first movement of Mozart's Flute Concerto No. 2. Please welcome Zach Gatalis!"

[PERFORMANCE OF MOZART]

DW [**milking applause for soloist**]: Zach Gatalis, everybody! We want to finish with one more great piece, the overture to the opera *Russlan and Lyudmila* by Russian composer Mikhail Glinka.

RJ: To make a long story short, *Russlan and Lyudmila* is a funny fairytale about a brave knight named Russlan who rescues Princess Lyudmila from an evil dwarf named Chernomore who has kidnapped her.

[BASS INSTRUMENT INTERRUPTS AND UNDERSCORES WITH *JAWS* LEITMOTIF; LIGHTING PROJECTS SHARK GOBO.]

RJ: Now wait a minute! I said an evil dwarf, not an evil shark! Let's have some evil dwarf music.

[ORCHESTRA PLAYS CHERNOMORE THEME; LIGHTING PROJECTS DWARF GOBO.]

RJ: That's more like it!

DW: Can you hear how that melody goes deeper and deeper? [sings and gestures with hands; gets audience to hum the theme] And the pitches have a certain tension to them; you can tell it's something bad.
Let's compare it to the melody of the brave knight Russlan.

[ORCHESTRA PLAYS RUSSLAN THEME; LIGHTING PROJECTS KNIGHT GOBO.]

RJ: Glinka uses the cellos, violas, and bassoons to show you how warmhearted Russlan is. Let's sing that theme together. [audience sings] Now listen how high-pitched instruments like the violins show what a cheerful, good person Princess Lyudmila is.

[ORCHESTRA PLAYS LYUDMILA; LIGHTING PROJECTS PRINCESS GOBO.]

DW: So listen for those melodies as the orchestra performs the Overture to *Russlan and Lyudmila*.

[ORCHESTRA PERFORMS GLINKA]

DW: So now you know how orchestras can use music to tell stories that are larger than life. We'd like to thank you all for being such wonderful listeners today. If you liked today's concert, tell your teachers and your parents because we'd love to see you at our next event. And, if any of you would like to learn to play these instruments, call the Bardavon to find out how you can take lessons from a Hudson Valley Philharmonic musician.

RJ: Now before you go, let's have one more big round of applause for today's legendary performers: Marietta Cheng, Zach Galatis, and the Hudson Valley Philharmonic!

From Discord, Find Harmony: A Musical Exploration of Conflict and Resolution

*F*rom Discord, Find Harmony: A Musical Exploration of Conflict and Resolution is another orchestral concert created for the Hudson Valley Philharmonic's *Classroom to Concert* program (see the introduction to *Myths and Legends* for a description of the context). This particular theme was suggested by several school teachers who had participated in Hudson Valley Philharmonic concerts the previous year. (In the postconcert evaluation forms, we always ask the teachers to suggest themes for the following year.) Because conflict resolution was a timely subject with rich musical implications, we enthusiastically embraced the suggestion. Our title came from Albert Einstein's Three Rules of Work: "Out of clutter find simplicity; from discord, find harmony; in the middle of difficulty lies opportunity."

Finding exciting repertoire proved to be an easy task, but choosing the best works and defining the right narrative approach required considerable work, discussion, and debate. Among the points that arose during the planning committee's philosophical discussions were the following:

- Conflict isn't always a bad thing; it's often unavoidable, and sometimes it's downright necessary.
- It's important to articulate the different kinds of conflict people can have in their lives and to find contrasting pieces that represent them.
- Most institutionalized conflict resolution operates under the assumption that people just need to sit down, share their points of view, listen to each other, and then everything will be fine and all of their problems will evaporate. Life often doesn't work that way. The context of our chosen repertoire definitely doesn't work that way.
- If we're doing a concert about conflict, we should engage the audience in a direct conflict within the first 30 seconds.

From Discord Find Harmony: A Musical Exploration of Conflict and Resolution—A Young People's Concert for the Hudson Valley Philharmonic

Marietta Cheng, conductor
David Wallace, musician and Teaching Artist
Kay Churchill, director of education
Chris Silva, producer and director

Program:
>   Leonard Bernstein: Overture to *West Side Story*
>   Pyotr Ilyich Tchaikovsky: *Romeo and Juliet Fantasy Overture*
>   Ludwig van Beethoven: Symphony No. 5 in C Minor I, III Bridge-IV
>   Camille Saint-Saëns: Concerto for Cello No. 1 in A Minor, Op. 33
>   Pyotyr Ilyich Tchaikovsky: *1812 Overture*

Materials:
>   Stage is set normally. Risers for winds and brass.
>   Eight large, colored sheets of poster board that form a spectrum above
>   the stage (they will be suspended from the ceiling). The four darkest
>   colors (black, blue, red, brown) will be house left. The four brightest
>   (green, day-glo pink, day-glo orange, day-glo yellow) will be house right.
>   Chair for David (doubles for cellist) that is stage right of the podium.
>   Police whistle for concertmaster Carol Cowan.
>   Miking: Lapel mike for David; Marietta prefers wireless normal mike,
>   which will be set on a stand behind her and used by David to go out into
>   the house.

David Wallace [DW] and Marietta Cheng [MC] enter from opposite sides of the stage. David divides the audience into two groups by drawing an invisible partition in the air. He motions to each group and indicates that house left side is with him, and house right side is with Marietta.

David gestures to show that he will do something, which will be echoed by his side, which will be echoed by Marietta, which will be echoed by her side.

David leads a simple four-beat call and response rhythm, which is echoed by his group, Marietta, and her group, respectively. This happens several times, then David looks at Marietta confrontationally and gets his group snapping a jazzy beat. Marietta returns David's challenging stance and summons her gang to start snapping the same beat.

DW: [to shortened WSS opening motive] We're better!

[HE GETS HIS GROUP LOOPING THIS MOTIVE OVER AND OVER]

MC: [to a slightly modified motivic response] No, you're not!

[ACCELERANDO AND MODEST CRESCENDO UNTIL CONCERTMASTER CAROL COWAN STANDS, BLOWS A POLICE WHISTLE, AND SIGNALS FOR EVERYONE TO STOP]

DW: Good morning, everybody! The Bardavon 1869 Opera House,
               Fleet Bank, and Texaco welcome you to this year's Hudson
               Valley Philharmonic Young People's Concert. I'm your host
               David Wallace, this is our marvelous conductor Marietta
               Cheng, and behind us are the spectacular musicians of the
               Hudson Valley Philharmonic.

Today's concert is all about conflict—arguments, struggles, battles. Music expresses conflict more powerfully than words. But music doesn't just leave us worked up and angry; it works through those feelings and resolves them.

We just used rhythm to create a conflict between two groups of people, and that's what the orchestra's first piece will be about.

MC: In a moment, we will hear music from *West Side Story* by the great American composer Leonard Bernstein. This music comes from a musical and movie about two New York City gangs, the Jets and the Sharks, who can't get along.

DW: To make the conflict worse, a guy name Tony, who used to be a Jet, falls in love with Maria, the sister of the leader of the Sharks.

MC: We'll hear music from three scenes: First we'll hear music for a fight, which is broken up by the police. Then we'll hear some lovely music that shows how Tony and Maria's hope and desire that things will work out. Finally, we'll hear music from a dance called the Mambo, where the Jets are trying to prove that they're even better dancers than the Sharks. Let's listen for these scenes in the overture to *West Side Story* by Leonard Bernstein.

[PERFORM OVERTURE TO *WEST SIDE STORY*]

DW: Those were some pretty exciting scenes! You could hear how the orchestra shows *West Side Story*'s conflict with all those exciting rhythms. Let's look at another way music can show conflict.

I have a question for you. How many of you have ever really wanted to do something that your parents wouldn't allow you to do? The next piece, *Romeo and Juliet Fantasy Overture* by Tchaikowsky, is about that kind of conflict. Most of you probably know the story.

Romeo and Juliet fall in love, but their families hate each other, so they won't let them be together. The music you will hear shows the conflicting feelings of love and hate. Just as in *West Side Story*, there will be some angry music to show the conflict between Romeo and Juliet's families, but there will be some beautiful music to show how badly Romeo and Juliet want to be together.

MC: Imagine you're a famous Hollywood composer and you've been asked to write music for a fight scene where there are lots of clashing swords? What kinds of instruments would you want to use? Yes? [trombones! drums!] Would you want the music to be loud or soft? [loud!] Fast or slow? [fast!] Smooth or rough? [rough!]

DW: Now, let's say you're asked to write music for a love scene. What kinds of instruments would you use? [violins. . . flute] Would you want the music to be soft or loud? [soft] Fast or slow? [slow] Smooth or rough? [smooth]

DW: Now we're going to improvise a little movie music. If I have my hand over my heart, I'd like you to play an imaginary violin and sing this smooth, soft, slow melody.

[DEMONSTRATES, SINGING STEPWISE MOTIVE FROM TCHAIKOVSKY, CUES, AND CUTS US OFF]

DW: Now, if I have my hand in a fist, play this loud, fast, rough, angry music on an imaginary trumpet.

[SINGS FIGURE FROM TCHAIKOWSKY. BRASS FANFARE, CUES, AND CUTS US OFF.]

MC: Let's go back to the two groups we had at the beginning of the concert. If I point to your group and have my hand over my heart, I want your section to play imaginary stringed instruments and hum that soft, slow, smooth music that shows Romeo and Juliet's love for each other. If I point to your side and hold my hand up in a fist, I want your section to play imaginary brass instruments and make some loud, angry, rough music that show the hate Romeo and Juliet's families have for each other.

[MC CONDUCTS A SHORT SOUND IMPROVISATION. DW PARTICIPATES AND ENCOURAGES THE GROUPS. RESOLVE THE IMPROVISATION WITH EVERYONE PLAYING LOVE MUSIC WITH A DIMINUENDO AL NIENTE.]

MC: Let's listen to the conflicting desires of love and hate in Tchaikowsky's *Romeo and Juliet Fantasy Overture.*

DW: If you hear the love theme, put your hand on your heart. If you hear conflict music, make a fist. Let's listen to hear if the piece ends with love or conflict.

[PERFORM *ROMEO AND JULIET FANTASY OVERTURE.* AS APPLAUSE DIES DOWN, IMMEDIATELY SEGUE INTO PERFORMANCE OF EXPOSITION OF THE FIRST MOVEMENT OF BEETHOVEN'S SYMPHONY NO. 5 IN C MINOR.]

DW: At the count of three, tell me who wrote this music. [He counts and cues; audience shouts "Beethoven!"] That's right, Ludwig van Beethoven! This is his Symphony No. 5 in C minor. Marietta, it sounded to me like this piece started with a conflict, but then it started to sound like things were being worked out. Could you tell us what's going on in this piece?

MC: In this piece, Beethoven wasn't writing about a conflict between families or gangs. He was writing about an inner conflict. As most of you know, at this point in his life,

Beethoven had almost entirely lost his hearing. This was a particularly cruel fate for a musician, and it created a great personal struggle for him. He once told a friend that these opening notes [She conducts orchestra which plays opening four notes] represent Fate knocking at the door.

DW: However, Beethoven decided that he would overcome this inner conflict by turning all of his attention and energy to creating great music. In this symphony, Beethoven uses the tone color of the harmonies and instruments of the orchestra to show his inner conflict and his overcoming it. Sometimes the music sounds very dark; sometimes it sounds very bright.

MC: You've probably noticed all the colors we have hanging from the ceiling. In a minute, instruments of the orchestra are going to play some different sounds, and without talking, I'd like you to point to the color that you think best represents the sound you hear.

What's an instrument that would be good at making some nice, rich, dark sounds? Yes? The cellos?

DW: Could we hear some dark sounds from the cellos?

[CELLOS PERFORM THEIR C MINOR BEETHOVEN EXCERPT. PROCESS IS REPEATED FOR THE AUDIENCE'S NEXT PICKS: BASSOON AND VIOLIN.]

MC: What's an instrument that could make some bright sounds? Piccolo? Let's hear that!

[AUDIENCE NEXT CHOOSES TRUMPET AND CYMBALS]

DW: Now Marietta and the orchestra are going to play some short parts of the Beethoven, and you point to the color that you think best represents the music you're hearing.

Let's hear some of Beethoven's darkest colors.

[ORCHESTRA PERFORMS EX. #1 III M. 324–331.]

DW: And some medium colors.

[ORCHESTRA PERFORMS EX #2 IV, M. 64–67; WOODWINDS ONLY.]

DW: And some of his brightest colors.

[FULL ORCHESTRA PERFORMS EX. #3 BEGINNING OF 4TH MOVEMENT (3¾ MEASURES)]

DW: Now with your hands down, let's listen to how Beethoven changes the tone color and harmony to show his dark struggle with fate and the bright sounds overcoming it.

[PERFORMANCE: ENTIRE 4TH MOVEMENT OF BEETHOVEN'S 5TH SYMPHONY; BEGIN FROM THE CODA OF THE 3RD MOVEMENT]

DW: Okay. So far we've heard music about conflicts between two gangs of people, music about the conflicting feelings of love and hate, and music about Beethoven's inner conflict with fate. Now, we're going to hear a piece of music representing a conflict between one person and the rest of the world.

MC: Have you ever had one of those bad days where everything goes wrong, and you feel like the whole world is out to get you? Well, this next piece is for you.

DW: In this next piece, the Concerto in A minor by Camille Saint-Saëns, a solo cellist, who represents the hero, will be performing against the background of the entire Hudson Valley Philharmonic Orchestra, which represents the rest of the world. Listen to see how this conflict works out. Will it get broken up by the police like in *West Side Story*? Does the hero fall in love like Romeo? Or does the hero triumph over his inner struggle like Beethoven?

MC: Playing cello today is the winner of this year's Virtuoso in Progress competition. This means he's one of the best young musicians in the entire Hudson Valley. He's a sixteen-year-old from Spackenkill High School. Please welcome Andy Choi!

[PERFORMANCE: FIRST MOVEMENT OF SAINT-SAËNS CELLO CONCERTO IN A MINOR]

DW [taking the wireless mic into the audience]: So who can tell me about the conflict they heard in this piece?

Audience Member #1: It sounded like there was this storm, and the hero had to get out of the storm, and then there was a battle.

DW: And what made it sound like a battle?

Audience Member #1: When the music was high and everybody was playing.

DW: And what did you hear?

Audience Member #2: It sounded like everybody was trying to get the cello, but in the end, the cello won anyway.

MC: Well, the final piece on today's concert is the *1812 Overture* by Tchaikowsky. This piece is about a real-life conflict between two nations. In 1812, a French general named Napoleon decided to invade Russia. You see, Napoleon was trying to take over all of Europe, and he almost succeeded. However, the Russians were able to fight off Napoleon's army, and Tchaikowsky's *1812 Overture* celebrates the Russians' triumph over the armies of Napoleon.

DW: To represent the French, Tchaikowsky uses the French national anthem.

[ORCHESTRA PERFORMS EXCERPT #4.]

MC: To represent the Russians, Tchaikowsky uses a proud Russian hymn to show that the Russians are ready to fight.

[ORCHESTRA PLAYS EXCERPT #5.]

DW: If you listen carefully, you will also hear these chimes which represent the Russians ringing church bells to warn everybody that the French are coming. The reason I have these mallets in my hands is that I'll be firing some cannon shots on the bass drum.

   Now, let me ask you something. How many of you on my side still think you're better than the kids on Marietta's side? [audience raises hands] How many of you on Marietta's side *know* that you're better than the kids on my side? Well, there's only one way to resolve this conflict! Whichever side listens the quietest, stillest, and notices the most details wins. Let's listen to the conflict between the Russians and the French in Tchaikowsky's *1812 Overture.*

[PERFORMANCE: *1812 OVERTURE*]

DW: So, let's see how you did. How many of you heard the French national anthem? the proud Russian hymn? the chimes? the cannon? Well, what do you think, Marietta?

MC: I think we resolved this conflict by proving that we're all outstanding listeners! Give each other a hand!

DW: Thank you all for being such wonderful musicians and listeners today. We hope you've learned how music can express conflicts and work them out. If you enjoyed today's concert, tell your teachers and your parents. We'd love to see you at our next concert, and we'd love for you to sign up for music lessons because almost all of us teach people how to play musical instruments. Now before you go, let's have one more big round of applause for Marietta Cheng, Andy Choi, and the Hudson Valley Philharmonic!

Improvisational Journey

Improvisational Journey is a solo concert I designed for myself and my own preferred repertoire. Although this concert began in elementary schools, I present it here as an example of an evening-length interactive concert suitable for a "grown-up" audience. Over dozens of performances, the concert has had several incarnations with varied formats, repertoire, and activities, most of which appear here. This transcript is drawn from multiple performances, but for convenience it shall be presented as though it all happened at the place my own interactive journey began: Saginaw, Michigan.

The concert was held at St. Stephen's Church, a Catholic church with modern architecture and reverberant, but clear acoustics. Seating is on one level in a somewhat semicircular pattern and sightlines are excellent throughout the sanctuary. The space accommodates approximately five hundred people. Multiple aisles give easy access to various parts of the sanctuary.

As you read, keep an eye out for various connections that were made to people in the community. Even if you are "just one musician," your residencies can involve far more people and organizations than you might first imagine.

Improvisational Journey

David Wallace, viola, violin, and piano
Luis Millan, guitar
The Saginaw Bay Youth Orchestra Chamber Group

Improvisation:
    J. S. Bach: Prelude in C Major
    Black-Key Improvisation
    Heinrich Biber: Passacaglia "The Guardian Angel"
    Georg Philipp Telemann: Viola Concerto in G Major

Intermission:
    Niccolo Paganini: Caprice #24
    Two Rounds of Texas-Style Contest Fiddling
    George Gershwin: "Summertime"
    Leroy Jenkins: *Viola Rhapsody, Big Wood, Festival Finale*

SPOKEN INTRODUCTION FROM SCOTT SEEBURGER OF DOW CORNING AND THE SAGINAW COMMUNITY ENRICHMENT COMMISSION.

Enter from the back of the hall and, without speaking, use body percussion to get the audience to perform layered rhythm patterns in the tempo of the Bach C major prelude. Pass out percussion instruments to volunteers who improvise rhythms over the layers (model it by jamming on each instrument while seeking a volunteer to take the instrument). Add in melodic vocal patterns if desired, and begin melodic improvisation in C on viola. Build the piece to a satisfying climax and conclusion. Youth orchestra musicians collect the instruments during applause.

David:	Good evening! Tonight we're going to take a journey into the world of musical improvisation. As we explore music spanning over 300 years, we'll discover the different shapes improvisation can take. But first, I'm going to ask you, "What is improvisation? How would you define it?"
Adult #1:	It's when you make something up off the top of your head.
David:	So, it's an act of spontaneous creation—
Adult #1:	Yes.
David:	Who can add to that?
Adult #2:	It could be like in jazz when a musician does a solo on a thirty-two-bar song.
David:	Tell me more about the solo part.
Adult #2:	Well, the rest of the band is playing the changes, but the person doing the solo is improvising on the chords or the melody.
David:	Ah, so there may be a background structure that underpins an improvisation. And one person may be featured while the others support him?
Adult #2:	Yes.
David:	And in the front row—what do you have to tell us?
Child #1:	There can be variations or decorations like ornaments and lots of times the audience claps to show that something's good.
David:	Great! What's your name?
Child #1:	Catherine.
David:	Catherine, where did you learn all that?
Child #1:	You came to my school and told us.
David:	Thank you for paying such close attention! Would you like to host the rest of the concert? [laughter]
	All that's been said is true. Improvisation is about creating in the moment, whether the improvisation is very free or highly structured. We began the evening by spontaneously creating a piece. Some of us were repeating very regular patterns, which we changed every now and then, and others were left to their own inspirations when they were given instruments. But in truth, we didn't know exactly what we would create; that's partly what makes improvisation exciting—not knowing exactly where the journey is going to take you.
	In the Baroque period in music, which lasted roughly from 1600 until 1750, musicians understood how exciting it

was to begin an event with an improvised piece of music. It was expected that musicians would begin a church service or a dance with an improvisation called a *prelude*. In time, many musicians actually began to write down their preludes, so we have a good idea of what these improvisations sounded like. I'm going to perform the prelude from the C major Cello Suite by Johann Sebastian Bach. This is how our evening might have begun if it were 1720, and I were the improvising musician preparing us for an evening of dance.

[PERFORM PRELUDE IN C ON VIOLA]

David: Although there's always an element of freedom and fantasy in Baroque preludes, you can hear that there's also a sense of order and structure.

[THE FOLLOWING IS PUNCTUATED WITH EXCERPTS FROM THE PRELUDE]

In this prelude, Bach is mostly playing around with scales— specifically scales in the key of C major . . . or when he's not playing scales, he's outlining harmonies. Sometimes he modulates to different keys—like he's taking us to a different setting or feeling, and sometimes he's just letting me show off a cool bowing effect.

So even within genres that suggest free improvisation, it's evident that musicians usually will focus on a handful of ideas and develop them one at a time within a given context. Now, I'm going to show you how *you* can do it.

How many of you have a piano or a keyboard instrument at home? I'll let you in on a secret that will enable you to improvise your own piano preludes—if you play only the black keys, you can never play a wrong note. Never! To prove that point, I'm even going to use my entire arm at some points to press about fifteen black keys at once. As long as you stay on the black keys, whatever you play will sound great. If you find a rhythm or a melody you like, do it again or change it a little until your fingers lead you to a new idea.

It can help if you have an idea about the larger structure, like knowing the feeling you want to express or thinking about what you want to do in terms of style or tempo. So I want you to give me some parameters for my "Black Key Prelude." Let's plan a scheme for the tempo. Contrast is always good, so I'd like to include sections of both fast and slow music. Who can suggest a plan for the tempos of the piece?

Adult #3: Start slow, then gradually build it until it's as fast as possible.

David: And how should it end?

Adult #3: With one big crash.

David: Okay. So here we go . . . slow-fast black-key improvisation culminating in one big crash!

[PERFORM BLACK-KEY IMPROVISATION ON PIANO]

David: So you can see that just with one or two little rules—like stay off the white keys, and gradually build the tempo—it's possible to improvise an interesting piece of music. The next time you find yourself at a piano, try this experiment. You'll be surprised at what you discover.

Free spontaneous creation is one end of the improvisation spectrum, but more often than not, improvisation happens within a set structure. One of the oldest and most common ways to improvise is to make up melodies over a repeating bass line. You can hear this in jazz, blues, *or* in an old dance from the Spanish Baroque called the *passacaglia*. Could everyone say "passacaglia"?

All: Passacaglia!

David: Good. In a passacaglia, there's a bass line that repeats over and over, and while that melody is repeating over and over, there's a lot of cool stuff that happens around that melody. But to really show you how a passacaglia works, we're going to create one together . . . let's get a beat going!

[BEGIN SNAPPING A STEADY BEAT, THEN BEGIN SINGING C-Bb-Ab-G ON THE SYLLABLE "DA." INDICATE FOR THE AUDIENCE TO JOIN IN. THEY CONTINUE SINGING WHILE I IMPROVISE VARIATIONS ABOVE THEM.]

David: Great singing! Let's give our improvised passacaglia a title . . . who can suggest a name?

Adult #4 (singing on the bass line): Down . . . the . . . moun . . . tain!

David: Nice. The "Down the Mountain" passacaglia by the Saginaw Community Singers and artist-in-residence. The passacaglia I'm about to perform for you has a title, too: "The Guardian Angel." What's a guardian angel?

Adult #5:   It's someone who protects you.

David: Is that a full-time or a part-time job?

Adult #5:   Full-time, I hope!

David: Full-time. In this passacaglia, that melody you all were singing "da-da-da-da" represents the continuous ongoing presence of the guardian angel. It's always there. Sometimes, it may be hard to hear it because of all the variations that are happening around it, but it's always there. So, if that melody is the guardian angel, what do you think the other music might represent?

Adult #6:   Evil.

Adult #7:   The devil.

Adult #8:   Temptation or trials.

Adult #9:   Danger.

Adult #10: The life of the person who's being protected.

David: So if you were a composer or improviser trying to represent the evil, danger, or temptations of a person going through life, what kinds of qualities would you want that music to have? What would it sound like? [write the suggestions down on a chart]

Adult #11: Dark, minor . . . dissonant chords.

David: So, harmonies with a dark, unsettled, or clashing quality.

Adult #12: I'd want plenty of contrasts.

David: Like what kind of contrasts?

Adult #12: Sometimes loud, sometimes soft. Sometimes fast, sometimes slow. Lots of surprises.

David: What else?

Adult #13: I'd have a lot of things going on at the same time to make it feel chaotic.

David: Good. I'm going to perform "The Guardian Angel" passacaglia for you, and I'd like you to do two things. First, see if you can hear the guardian angel, the "da-da-da-da" melody. No matter how much is going on, it's *always* there, except for one place where it stops and I improvise a short solo called a cadenza. Secondly, notice all the different ways the music shows all the trials, dangers, and temptations of the person's journey. Here's "The Guardian Angel" passacaglia written in 1675 by the German violinist and composer Heinrich Biber.

[PERFORM BIBER'S PASSACAGLIA]

David: So, let's see a show of hands—how many of you heard the guardian angel melody most of the time except for during the cadenza? And how many could hear it all the time? Great. What were some of the ways Biber showed a person going through all of life's dangers, evils, and temptations?

Adult #14: Some really fast notes!

David: Absolutely. [plays a measure of a fast variation and adds "fast notes" to the list] What else?

Adult #15: Sometimes it was actually very soft and comforting.

David: Yes, almost as though the person finds security in the presence of the angel. [plays a softer variation and adds the new thought to the list] Let's go through the rest of our predictions—did we hear dark, minor, or dissonant chords? contrasts in volume and tempo? surprises? many things going on to suggest chaos? Excellent. So you can see how much possibility there is for creating music above a repeating bass line, and that's why it's been a favorite technique of improvising musicians for centuries.

          So we began our concert by exploring essentially free improvisation, then we experienced improvisation over a bass line, and now we'll move to one of the most structured forms of improvisation: ornamentation. As the name suggests, ornamentation is really about decorating preexisting melodies by improvising embellishments. This was a widespread practice in Bach and Biber's day; it was rare for musicians to perform the music exactly as it was written.

[MEMBERS OF THE SAGINAW BAY YOUTH ORCHESTRA CHAMBER GROUP WALK ONSTAGE]

David: I'm going to play a few ornaments, and I'm going to ask you to draw a shape in the air that represents the sound of the ornament. Here's a popular ornament called a trill. I see some of you doing zigzag lines; some composers actually used that symbol to show a trill. Sometimes musicians would make very quick, sharp trills called mordents. Let's see how you would draw that . . . look around and see what you see others doing. Here's another ornament called a turn. And sometimes musicians would just decorate a melody with passing notes and scales.

Luis Millan and the Saginaw Bay Youth Orchestra Chamber Group are joining me now. We're going to perform the Viola Concerto in G Major by Georg Philipp Telemann. This was written in 1730, and to our knowledge, it's the world's first solo viola concerto. It was quite possibly the first instance of a violist getting to stand in front of an orchestra and improvise.

You probably noticed all these giant, decorated Telemann viola concerto scores we've posted on the walls of the church. As I toured the schools during each concert, I would play an unornamented version of the first movement of this concerto while a few students decorated the score of it with artwork and the kinds of ornamentation symbols you were drawing in the air. Then I would repeat the movement again, using these decorations as a springboard for my improvised ornaments. [pointing to a wildly decorated version] This version was particularly challenging!

So if I just take the first solo viola phrase and play it without any ornamentation, it sounds like this. [play the opening line of the viola solo] But when I read *this* decorated score and play it with these butterflies and curlicues, it sounds like . . . [play ornamented version]

Is there a student here who remembers what we talked about when we compared the ornamented version to the unornamented version?

Child #2: The first way was like a cake without frosting, and second way was like a cake with frosting.

David: And which one did you like better?

Child #2: The second one!

David: Me, too. Tonight, I'll be taking the best ideas from the decorated scores that you see, and use them as a basis for my improvised ornaments as we perform Telemann's Viola Concerto in G Major. Keep your ears open for moments where the orchestra stops and I have to improvise a cadenza. Enjoy!

[PERFORM TELEMANN VIOLA CONCERTO IN G MAJOR]

David: We're going to take a ten-minute intermission, but don't go away because when you come back, we'll take improvisation out of the German Baroque and into the realm of violin pyrotechnics, Texas-style fiddling, and jazz! Let's have one more round of applause for Luis Millan and the brilliant young musicians of the Saginaw Bay Youth Orchestra Chamber Group!

INTERMISSION

[AS THE LIGHTS DIM, ENTER FROM THE WINGS AND PERFORM PAGANINI, CAPRICE #24 WHILE TRAVELING THROUGH AUDIENCE]

David: That was the 24th caprice of Italian violinist Niccolo Paganini, who was such an amazing violinist and improviser that he was rumored to have sold his soul to the Devil in exchange for his incredible talent. As he toured Europe, he often would include an improvised theme and variations as part of his concert or as an encore. He would take a popular melody—a theme— and then play several different versions of it. Mozart, Haydn, and Beethoven had done this before him, so it really wasn't a new concept, but what was new were some of the special effects he could make on his violin.

Let's break down what he did. Everybody here knows "Yankee Doodle," right? [play "Yankee Doodle" melody] I'm going to use that for my theme. Now, let's make up some variations based on some of the innovative effects you heard in the 24th caprice. What was something that you noticed me doing in the caprice?

Adult #16: There was that plucking part.

David: Yes, he did a pizzicato, or plucking variation. If we did something similar in "Yankee Doodle," it would sound like this. [demonstrate] What else did you hear?

Adult #17: I heard an almost violent part where you were going like [gestures].

David: [plays the beginning of the triple stop variation] Like this?

Adult #17: Yes.

David: That would be chords. If we do that to "Yankee Doodle," you would get [play chordal variation on "Yankee Doodle"]. What else did you hear?

Adult #18: There were some fast scales.

David: Yes, almost like he had taken a lesson from Heinrich Biber's passacaglia. If we put some fast scales into a "Yankee Doodle" variation, you might have something like [improvise fast scalar variation]. Let me show you one other technique where he lightly touches the string to make ultra-high-pitched sounds called harmonics. [demonstrate a phrase of the harmonics variation] If I do that to "Yankee Doodle," you'll hear something like [create a harmonics variation]. So, I'm going to make up Paganini-style theme and variations on "Yankee Doodle." First, I'll play the melody, then I'll play a pizzicato variation, a chords variation, a variation with fast scales, a harmonics variation, and maybe one or two more for good measure. Here we go . . .

[PERFORM A THEME AND VARIATIONS ON "YANKEE DOODLE"]

David: Now, let's hear Paganini's 24th Caprice again, but this time, listen to it as a series of variations, each based around a particular technique.

[PERFORM CAPRICE #24]

David: I'm going to invite guitarist Luis Millan back to the stage to join me for this next segment, and we're going to perform two rounds of Texas-style contest fiddling. I grew up in Texas where they have a very rich musical tradition that grew out of competitions where people would come from all over the nation to prove who was the best fiddler. Texas-style fiddling includes many of the improvisational techniques we've explored tonight, and it's a particularly interesting style because it is a melting pot of genres and improvisational techniques from around the world.

Most of the fast tunes are variations that happen over a repeated bass line. [Luis performs a sixteen-bar walking bass progression in A major with jazz harmonies] It's a little jazzier and more complex than Biber's guardian angel theme, but it serves the same function.

I'll be using quite a bit of ornamentation, only instead of being the kinds of ornaments you would find in the German Baroque, I'll play trills, rolls, graces, and triplets derived from Irish and Scottish fiddling. [punctuate with demonstrations of each]

And while I'll be creating variations, instead of using Paganini's pyrotechnic techniques, I'll be using techniques that developed in American fiddling like fourth-finger drones, or creating variations in a higher position, or adding in some jazzy blue notes. [punctuate with demonstrations of each]

Now, so far, you've been a very polite audience, and have listened very well and attentively, but I'm going to ask you to behave like an audience at a Texas fiddle contest. At a fiddle contest, when a performer does something really interesting, the audience will spontaneously applaud or yell encouragement.

Let's practice; let's say you were really impressed with a variation I just played, so you decide to applaud for about five seconds . . . ready? Go! Alright, now let's do that again, but yell, "Whoo!"

Wonderful! Now let me just hear you say, "Hey-hey! Yeah!" Good! I think you're ready.

Make me work for your cheers, though. Don't respond unless you hear something really great, and do it only a couple of times per tune.

We'll play you two contest rounds. At a Texas-style fiddle contest, you're required to play three tunes per round: a breakdown, which is basically a very jazzy, improvisatory reel; a waltz, and a tune-of-choice *other* than a breakdown or waltz. The tune-of-choice may be a polka, a schottische, a hornpipe, a swing tune, a rag, or none-of-the-above. So, here's a contest round. The breakdown will be "Tom & Jerry"; the waltz is "Wednesday Night Waltz," and the tune-of-choice will be a quick Mexican polka called "Jesse Polka."

PERFORM CONTEST ROUND #1

David: Thank you! We're going to play another round, since it sounds like we passed that one! The breakdown for the second round will be "Billy in the Lowground," which goes all the way back to 17th-century Scotland. There's a story—probably apocryphal—that there was a farmer named Billy who was farming the lowlands by the river, and he fell into a deep pit. For some reason—don't ask me why—he happened to have his fiddle with him. The variations represent his fiddling for help.

While you listen to this breakdown, I'd like you to notice another element of the Texas style. One thing that distinguishes it from bluegrass and other folk styles is that the improvisation is really driven by a 3+3+2 cross rhythm. Instead of going *ta-ka-ta-ka ta-ka-ta-ka* like most fiddle music or classical music, it subdivides the beat with a jazzy rhythm: *ba-da-da ba-da-da da-da!* **one**-two-three **one**-two-three- **one**-two! Try that: *ba-da-da ba-da-da da-da!* [have the audience loop the cross-rhythm and then play a phrase or two over it]

That's the basic groove. You could hear when I added melody that I was often looping three-note patterns with you; that's what's called a riff. And in Texas, they love to riff on this breakdown. Here's "Billy in the Lowground."

[PERFORM "BILLY IN THE LOWGROUND"]

David: Next, we'll play a Canadian waltz that is usually called—oddly enough—"Canadian Waltz." The original name was actually

"Ookpik Waltz," probably named after Ookpik the Arctic owl, which Luis is holding up right now. This doll and character became a national trademark for Canadian handicrafts during the 1960s; that's a vintage Ookpik doll I found on an internet auction. The waltz itself is rather somber because it uses some blue notes and the kind of ornamentation that you might find in Scottish airs and ballads.

[PERFORM "CANADIAN WALTZ"]

David: We'll finish the round with a ragtime tune that was originally a piano rag by Iowan composer George Botsford: the "Black and White Rag."—You'll really hear the *ba-da-da ba-da-da da-da!* cross-rhythms in this one. Every now and then, Luis is going to stop, and I'll play a short solo called a "break." Breaks were common in early jazz and swing. They're similar to the Baroque cadenzas you heard in the Biber and the Telemann, only this time, they're very rhythmic and happen in the span of four beats. In the school concerts, the kids got to improvise breaks in the moment, but tonight, I'll do the honors.

[PERFORM "BLACK AND WHITE RAG"]

David: Thank you. We're going to continue in a jazzy vein with a standard that is a favorite of Texas fiddlers and jazz musicians alike: George Gershwin's "Summertime." As someone mentioned at the beginning of the concert, jazz musicians will often improvise a solo over the chord changes of a song. The solo may be based on the melody, or it may depart from it. In a band situation, everybody takes a solo, but first, the tune is presented by the singer or a melody instrument, and usually at the end the tune comes back as well.

Since I'm sure most of us know the song, let's sing the first verse together. Then Luis will take a solo, I'll take a solo, then let's finish with the second verse. Luis?

[LUIS PLAYS INTRO; PERFORM "SUMMERTIME" AS A SING-ALONG]

David: I'm going to finish tonight's concert with a set of pieces by Leroy Jenkins, who was one of the pioneers of avant-garde jazz violin. I moved to Brooklyn about a year ago, and by a miraculous coincidence, my new home was only a few doors down from Leroy's. He stopped me on the street one day and said, "Hey, are you that violinist who lives on Prospect Place? Come on over sometime, and I'll show you some tunes!"

The first piece I'm going to perform is called *Viola Rhapsody*. As with most of Leroy's compositions, I'll play a composed section, then improvise freely within the context and parameters he gives me. This particular piece alternates chords and harmonies with smooth melodic lines. I want to take you inside the harmonies, so let's divide the audience into three sections. Okay, if you're in this section, your part is this: "Do---- Fa---- Do---- Sol----" Let's try it . . . Good!

Now, if you're in the middle, your part goes like this: "Mi---- Fa---- Mi---- Re----." Sing with me . . . great!

And if you're on this side, you'll have the soprano line that goes like this: "Sol---- La---- Sol---- Fa----." Everybody!

Great. Now, let's put all three parts together and I'll play the same chords on viola with what's called a ricochet bowing. Sustain your notes and watch the scroll of my viola for the changes.

Okay, there's still something missing; if this is jazz, there has to be some improvisation, right? Raise your hand if you play piano. Wow! That's a lot of players . . . sir, could you help me out? What I need you to do is sit at the piano, and play some smooth, flowing notes on the white keys. We'll play our chords, pause and let you take a turn, and we'll come back in and keep taking turns. It's impossible for you to make a mistake; just play some smooth and flowing notes. Game? Great; give our volunteer a hand! So, let's make a viola-piano-vocal rhapsody. Here we go . . .

[PERFORM IMPROVISATION]

David: Wonderful! Give yourselves a hand. So in *Viola Rhapsody*, Leroy asks me to play the chords you just learned, then I have to play a double-stop melody that sounds like this [play a few bars of middle section], then I'm on my own. He says, "Play chords until you can't play any more chords, then play melody until you can't play any more melody. Just keep alternating." Listen for how much variety can be found just within those two ways of playing. Here's *Viola Rhapsody*.

[PERFORM *VIOLA RHAPSODY*]

David: The next work, *Big Wood*, was written for solo viola and improvised modern dance. In the school tours, children have actually been improvising dance to my performance, but tonight, we have the privilege of enjoying the improvised choreography of dancers from Saginaw High School. Please give them a warm welcome!

This particular piece uses some of Jenkins's most unusual sound effects, and the dancers have to react accordingly, as they'll demonstrate. Sometimes, I have to make some harsh scratching sounds with the bow—watch how the dancers react. Other times, I'm playing a fast trill while bowing on the bridge to make a raspy sound. Listen for those and many other effects as the dancers and I perform *Big Wood*.

[PERFORM *BIG WOOD*]

David: Thank you. I'm going to conclude the concert with Leroy Jenkins's *Festival Finale*, but first I'd like to say a word of thanks to Scott Seeburger of Dow Corning, and Nancy Koepke and Barb Day of the Saginaw Community Enrichment Commission for making this residency so enjoyable. I'd also like to thank all of you for coming out tonight; you've been an extraordinary audience—especially those of you who are missing the first half of the Red Wings playoff game! Here's Leroy Jenkins's *Festival Finale!*

[PERFORM *FESTIVAL FINALE*]

Appendix B
Interactive Concert Checklist

SCRIPTING AND ACTIVITY DESIGN CHECKLIST:

Does the concert have:

____ a nice overall arch and shape and a good program order?

____ appropriate pacing of musical works and interactions?

____ a culminating piece or activity?

____ a good balance between performance and interaction (approximately two-thirds music one-third interaction)?

____ intentional decisions about theatrical elements (set, lighting, blocking, etc.)?

Do we:

____ engage the audience as listeners, cocreators, and coperformers?

____ offer a variety of activity types?

____ offer a variety of activity formats (whole group, a few volunteers, etc.)?

____ address multiple intelligences and modes of perception?

____ include at least one visual aid or visual activity?

____ provide effective transitions from one part to the next?

Do the interactions:

____ provide opportunities for reflection?

____ provide clear entry points and listening foci for every piece?

____ have a significant payoff that makes them worthwhile to the audience?

____ enhance the hearing of the music?

PREPARATION AND LOGISTICS CHECKLIST:

Have we:

____ completely scripted the concert?

____ refined the wording to achieve maximum clarity and conciseness?

____ memorized our script and outline?

____ rehearsed the script and the blocking as seriously as the music?

____ made all performers aware of their roles?

____ tried out the interactions on friends or held an open dress rehearsal?

____ notified our venue's management, stagehands, lighting or technical crews of any needs?

____ [if the event is a school concert] written and sent a teachers' guide containing information about our group, the concert, the pieces, the composers? Does this guide include simple activities that will enhance our concert?

____ Made arrangements to have our concert recorded or videoed?

ASSESSMENT AND POSTCONCERT REFLECTION:

____ Have we made simple assessment forms for our audiences to fill out so we can have valuable constructive feedback and useful quotes for our press kit?

____ Do we have trustworthy, objective friends to attend and give feedback?

____ Have we set a time to watch the concert video and evaluate it?

Appendix C
Annotated Bibliography

Following are some of the sources that have influenced my approach and development as a Teaching Artist and interactive performer. I trust you will find them useful and that you will explore the additional resources that are emerging as our field develops.

Bernstein, Leonard. *Leonard Bernstein's Young People's Concerts*. Edited by Jack Gottlieb. New York: Anchor Books, 1992.

This book contains some of Bernstein's greatest scripts and is well worth study. While you're at it, be sure to visit www.leonardbernstein.com where you can order DVDs of the Young People's Concerts and read his scripts online.

Booth, Eric. *The Everyday Work of Art*. Naperville, Ill.: Sourcebooks, Inc., 1997.

One of the first books on aesthetic education to cross over into the public marketplace, *The Everyday Work of Art* examines the tools and strategies artists use in their work. The book includes numerous practical exercises and examples so that readers can apply the skills of art-making to everyday life.

Cabaniss, Thomas. "A Teaching Artist Prepares." *Teaching Artist Journal* 1, no. 1 (2003): 31–37.

This groundbreaking article is a wonderful and detailed description of the process of brainstorming a work of art and designing teaching activities.

Education Concert Rubric. New York: The American Symphony Orchestra League, 2004.

To help orchestras and musicians to develop the best possible interactive concerts, the American Symphony Orchestra League created a rubric for assessing the quality of programming, scripting, audience engagement, and script delivery/performance. This phenomenal document and other useful materials may be downloaded from the ASOL website (www.symphony.org).

Flagg, Aaron, Ani Gregorian, Sarah Johnson, and David Wallace. *New York Philharmonic: Bernstein Live!: New York Philharmonic Special Edition for Teachers, Vol. 2*. New York: New York Philharmonic Society, 2002.

President and executive director Zarin Mehta writes, "With this second volume of Special Edition for Teachers, we are proud to provide teachers and students with inspired presentations of exceptional live performances by Leonard Bernstein. In his tradition of communicating the joy of music to audiences of all ages, the lessons in this volume will allow you and your students to share in his incomparable musical legacy." Using multiple intelligences and tried and true activities, this volume presents additional examples of workshops for exploring musical works. Available at www.nyphilharmonic.org.

Flagg, Aaron, Thomas Cabaniss, and David Wallace. *New York Philharmonic: An American Celebration: New York Philharmonic Special Edition for Teachers, Vol. 1.* New York: New York Philharmonic Society, 2001.

President and executive director Zarin Mehta writes, "With this Special Edition for Teachers, we are proud to make vibrant examples of the American orchestral repertoire available to teachers and students in ways that engage, involve, and inspire." This book and companion CD contain activities and lessons that demonstrate how to build more extensive preparatory workshops around entry points into a particular piece of music. Available at www.nyphilharmonic.org.

Gardner, Howard. *Multiple Intelligences: The Theory in Practice.* New York, N.Y.: Basic Books, 1993.

Every educator should be familiar with Howard Gardner's multiple intelligence theory and its practical application. While there are many authors on the subject, it's always good to go to the primary source.

Green, Barry, with W. Timothy Gallwey. *The Inner Game of Music.* Garden City, N.Y.: Doubleday, 1986.

Barry Green's insightful book contains many strategies for enjoying music as well as conquering stage fright and musical challenges. His clear principles are easily transferable to teaching and interacting with an audience.

Highstein, Ellen. *Making Music in Looking Glass Land: A Guide to Survival and Business Skills for the Classical Musician.* New York, N.Y.: Concert Artists Guild, 1997.

Making Music in Looking Glass Land is a Bible for any ensemble or musician pursuing a freelance concert career. Highstein gives practical advice on management, booking, promotion, and other essential aspects of building a performing career.

Marsalis, Wynton. *Marsalis on Music.* 216 min. Sony Wonder. Videocassette (ASIN 6303640362), 1995.

Wynton Marsalis is a charismatic musical ambassador with a heart for teaching. These videos provide us with an exceptional role model who has a natural approach for sharing music with young people.

Pathways to the Orchestra. Thomas Cabaniss and David Wallace, editors. New York: The New York Philharmonic Society, 2002.

Written by eleven Teaching Artists in collaboration with five classroom teachers, this three-year curriculum is chockfull of ideas for activities and entry points into musical masterpieces. At the time of this publication, *Pathways to the Orchestra* is available for download at the teacher resources section at www.nyphilharmonic.org.

Taylor, Livingston. *Stage Performance.* New York: Pocket Books, 2000.

Singer, songwriter, and Berklee College of Music professor Livingston Taylor shares his wisdom about serving and captivating an audience. His brother James embodies his advice.